on screen ...
David Cronenberg

every movie, every star

Patrick Chapman

SONIC**BOND**

sonicbondpublishing.com

Sonicbond Publishing Limited
www.sonicbondpublishing.co.uk
Email: info@sonicbondpublishing.co.uk

First Published in the United Kingdom 2021
First Published in the United States 2021

British Library Cataloguing in Publication Data:
A Catalogue record for this book is available from the British Library

Copyright Patrick Chapman 2021

ISBN 978-1-78952-071-2

Typeset in ITC Garamond & ITC Avant Garde
Printed and bound in England

Graphic design and typesetting: Full Moon Media

on screen ...
David Cronenberg

every movie, every star

Patrick Chapman

sonicbondpublishing.com

To Seán A., since the year of *The Fly*.

Contents

David Cronenberg ... *On Screen*

Introduction

This book invites newcomers and fans alike to discover or revisit the cinema of David Cronenberg. It is the first to discuss his entire filmography, from *Transfer* (1966) to *Maps to the Stars* (2014), as well as covering other aspects of his career: shorts, television, commercials, acting, writing and exhibitions.

There is a lot to explore. Some of Cronenberg's art approaches genius, some of it does not, but whatever your view on his achievement, it is a fascinating body of work. Political, philosophical, sometimes darkly funny, often quite disturbing: here is a cinema like no other. Your reaction will depend both on what you bring to his films, and what they bring out in you.

Enter the world of David Cronenberg and you discover a cinematic universe filled with terror and wonder, big ideas and small parasites, open minds and opened bodies, sometimes all in the same scene. Transgressive and moral, horrific and fearless, Cronenberg contains multitudes.

From his earliest days as a filmmaker he has had original things to say, usually expressed with a deadpan sense of the absurd, his work reflecting the human condition by holding up a mirror that is sometimes distorted yet always true.

Starting out in a genre that critics tended not to take seriously, he showed that real horror comes from within, and you can probably have sex with it. Here was a director interested in our potential for change – in all sorts of ways – but some dismissed him as merely a 'baron of blood'. Cronenberg's dedication to his own path has long since been vindicated. Feted by festivals, adored by many critics, he is now regarded as one of our greatest film directors. Not only is the adjective 'Cronenbergian' an aspirational byword for a particular sensibility, the word 'cronenberg' has become both a verb and a noun. While unashamedly celebrating genre, this director has always been *sui generis*. Whether working from a self-written script or adapting someone's book, he holds to Burroughs's idea that 'nothing is true, everything is permitted'. Thrilling to those who appreciate it, this can provoke outrage in moral guardians who may not have seen the film in question but are certain that 'something must be done'.

Cronenberg's cinema is personal by necessity. He chooses projects that allow him to investigate his own obsessions and themes: infection as catalyst, creatively destructive change, our merging with technology, and the inner drives that transform us. He turned down the job of directing *Return of the Jedi* because he 'wasn't used to doing other people's material'. Still, he changed his mind when the right story came along. In 1983, the year that *Jedi* opened, he released a melancholy adaptation of Stephen King's *The Dead Zone*, as well as a self-penned masterpiece, *Videodrome*. *The Shape of Rage*, the first book to study his work, was published that year as part of a festival retrospective. A mere seventeen years after he shot his first frame, David Cronenberg had become an overnight success.

If the nominally mainstream *The Dead Zone* was his flirtation with a mass audience, his next film took them dancing on the ceiling. Quintessentially

Cronenberg, *The Fly* (1986) remains his most commercially successful release. A gory SF-horror, it is also a moving allegory of disease, transition and interspecies love. Its lead actors, Jeff Goldblum and Geena Davis, were a couple in real life, and that chemistry shines through in their performances.

Hovering near the midpoint of his filmography, between the early, semi-exploitation horrors and his late-career run of acclaimed literary dramas, *The Fly* is an ideal gateway drug for the curious viewer new to Cronenberg.

On the other hand, you may wish to take the chronological route, starting with his early shorts and following the evolution of his films, then reading his novel, *Consumed*.

For your viewing pleasure, this book includes a guide to current physical releases of the films, some of which offer restored prints and useful supplementary material. There is also a bibliography for further reading.

Due to the nature of Cronenberg's work, a trigger warning seems to be in order. Here it is: be afraid, be very afraid, of spoilers. If in doubt, watch first and read later.

Viewing Guide

The best place to see David Cronenberg's work is on a cinema screen, although the early films are well suited to home video. The director himself is not particularly worried about where his films are seen, given how good domestic setups have become, and how the light from cell-phone screens detracts from the experience in cinemas.

This is a list of good-to-excellent physical releases current at the time of going to press. Please check that the region codes and formats are compatible with your equipment.

Transfer, From the Drain, Stereo, Crimes of the Future. Released as *David Cronenberg's Early Works*, Arrow Video Blu-ray, 2016. In the US, the two shorts also appear on Blue Underground's 2009 Blu-ray of *Fast Company*.

Camera, At the Suicide of the Last Jew in the World in the Last Cinema in the World, The Nest. All included as extras on Turbine Media's 2020 Blu-ray of *Crash. Camera* is an extra on Arrow's 2015 Blu-ray release of *Videodrome. At the Suicide...* is part of *Chacun Son Cinéma*, a film commissioned to celebrate 60 years of the Cannes Film Festival.

Shivers
US: Vestron Video Blu-ray, 2020.
UK: Arrow Video Blu-ray/DVD, 2014.
France: *Frissons*, ESC Editions Blu-ray/DVD, 2020.

Rabid
US: Scream Factory Blu-ray, 2016.
UK: Arrow Video Blu-ray, 2014.

Fast Company
US: Blue Underground Blu-ray, 2009.
Germany: Endless Classics Blu-ray, 2017.

The Brood
US: The Criterion Collection Blu-ray, 2015.
Germany (Die Brut): Wicked-Vision Media Blu-ray, 2019

Scanners
US: The Criterion Collection Blu-ray/DVD, 2014.
UK: Second Sight Blu-ray, 2013.

Videodrome
US: The Criterion Collection Blu-ray, 2010.
UK: Arrow Video Blu-ray, 2015.

The Dead Zone
Germany: Koch Media Blu-ray, 2018.
Spain: *La Zona Muerta*, Selecta Blu-ray, 2020.

The Fly
US: As part of *The Fly Collection* Scream Factory Blu-ray, 2020.
US: Standalone: Fox Blu-ray, 2007.
UK: Fox Blu-ray, 2008.

Dead Ringers
US: Scream Factory Blu-ray, 2016.
UK: ITV Studios Blu-ray, 2018.
Germany: *Die Unzertrennlichen*, Koch Media Blu-ray, 2018.

Naked Lunch
US: The Criterion Collection Blu-ray, 2013.
Germany: Studiocanal Blu-ray, 2015.

M. Butterfly
US: Warner Archive DVD, 2006.
Germany: Warner DVD, 2006.

Crash
Germany: Turbine Media Group Blu-ray, 2020
UK: Arrow Video Blu-ray, 2020
US: Criterion Collection Blu-ray, 2020.

eXistenZ
US: Miramax EchoBridge Blu-ray, 2012.
UK: 101 Films, Black Label Blu-ray, 2018.

Spider
US: Sony DVD, 2003.
UK: Lionsgate DVD, 2008.

A History of Violence
US: Miramax EchoBridge Blu-ray, 2012.
UK: Entertainment in Video Blu-ray, 2018.

Eastern Promises
US: Universal Pictures Blu-ray, 2008.
UK: Fox Blu-ray 2008.

A Dangerous Method
US: Sony Blu-ray, 2012.
UK: Lionsgate Blu-ray, 2012.

Cosmopolis
US: Entertainment One Blu-ray, 2016.
UK: Entertainment One Blu-ray, 2012.

Maps to the Stars
US: Universal Pictures Blu-ray, 2015.
UK: Entertainment One Blu-ray, 2015.

A History of Cronenberg

What shapes an artist? If one produces work that society considers transgressive, does it spring from a personality disorder, or from a life that is less than impeccable? Some argue for the inciting event that sets someone on the path to a future as director, writer, musician, sculptor, or painter. In the case of David Cronenberg, the nightmare fuel seems to have been that least obvious of motivations, a happy, nurturing childhood. 'Be steady and well-ordered in your life so that you can be fierce and original in your work', Flaubert said. Cronenberg would appear to be an exemplar of that. His demons are the ones he creates.

Born on 15 March 1943 in Toronto, Ontario, future filmmaker David Paul Cronenberg grew up in a comfortable, middle class, progressive Jewish family. His Canadian mother, Esther, née Sumberg, was a pianist for the National Ballet, as well as a music teacher. His American father, Milton, was a writer, editor and philatelist who hailed from Baltimore and had run a bookshop earlier in life. His grandparents on both sides had emigrated from Lithuania. His sister Denise would become a costume designer, celebrated for her work on her brother's films, as well as others.

Young David's upbringing was a liberal one in a house filled with books. As he told New York magazine in 2005, 'We had a huge collection of books – other kids were amazed. They had maybe one book at their house, the Bible or something, and we had walls of books'. In the same interview, he mentioned his boxes of comics, including the darker-themed EC books. He also spoke about the science fiction authors he read, one of whom was Isaac Asimov. 'He was important, a legitimate scientist and an artist – a writer – at the same time'. Interestingly, given that they have explored similar themes, and he once tried to make *Total Recall*, he didn't read Philip K. Dick until he was older.

The interests that he developed as a boy would go on to inform his career. David wrote all the time: stories, plays, fantasies. He sent some off to SF magazines and received encouraging rejections. His penchant for writing, along with his interest in science, might suggest an identification with the young Mantle twins at the start of *Dead Ringers* but that would be too easy. The artist is not necessarily the art. Famously, Martin Scorsese saw *Shivers* at Cannes in 1975 and was shaken. Cronenberg found this ironic: 'You're the guy who made *Taxi Driver* and you're afraid to meet me?'

At high school, he pursued the sciences, particularly botany and lepidopterology. Taking Honours Science at the University of Toronto in 1963, he switched a year later to Honours English, his twin muses becoming conjoined. Similarly, J. G. Ballard, whose novel *Crash* Cronenberg would adapt, studied medicine before his literary career began.

Two formative events turned this bookish child towards the cinema. One was seeing patrons overcome with weeping while leaving the local movie house, the Pylon on College Street. He learned that these Italian immigrants had been to see *La Strada* and had found it deeply emotional. On seeing it himself,

David also wept, and discovered that the moving image was called that for a reason. The second crucial experience was seeing a film in college, by one of his contemporaries: David Secter's *Winter Kept Us Warm* (1965). Shot when its director was twenty-two, this was Canada's first overtly LGBTQ-themed film. It was also the first English-language Canadian film screened at Cannes. In *Cronenberg on Cronenberg*, edited by Chris Rodley, the director says that 'Secter had somehow hustled together a feature film that was intriguing because it was completely unprecedented. And then the film appeared, and I was stunned. Shocked. Exhilarated. It was an unbelievable experience. This movie was a very sweet film... That was my awareness of film as something that I could do.' It was, he later said, the most influential film of his life, 'in a weird way'.

The place of *Winter Kept Us Warm* in film history is significant; in a 2005 documentary, several cultural figures, including Cronenberg, discussed its importance.

Now the fledgeling director had found motivation. He rented cameras and experimented with the available technology. He learned how to make films and soon had produced two 16mm shorts. Coming across as absurdist theatre pieces put on film, *Transfer* (1966) and *From the Drain* (1967) displayed his penchant for non-naturalistic storytelling and dry humour.

Around this time, inspired by Jonas Mekas' underground film group in New York, Cronenberg formed the Toronto Film Co-op with Iain Ewing and Ivan Reitman. Ewing had appeared in David Secter's feature.

On returning from a year in France – where among other things he made a sculpture called *Surgical Instrument for Operating on Mutants* – Cronenberg returned to the University of Toronto. He graduated at the top of his class.

Although at one time he had aspired to become a novelist, his interest in film took over in earnest with his first short feature, an hour-long black-and-white art-film, *Stereo* (1969). Featuring the sterile, brutalist architecture of the Toronto University campus, this, along with his next picture, *Crimes of the Future* (1970), took influences from Cronenberg's reading of science fiction. The first of his unusually named characters and institutions appear at this point (The Canadian Academy of Erotic Enquiry in *Stereo*; Adrian Tripod in *Crimes*). There are also premonitions of themes that recur in his professional films, including ambivalence towards psychotherapy, a monstrous threat coming out of a drain, and psychic abilities unlocked through disfigurement. *Scanners* works as a spiritual follow-up to *Stereo*.

Not satisfied with making films that were more likely to run in a gallery than in the other kind of picture house, Cronenberg wanted as wide a viewership as possible. His next move would bring him into the arena of exploitation cinema, a route taken before him by Coppola, De Palma and Scorsese.

In 1972, he married Margaret Hindson, who had worked on some of his experimental projects. Their marriage would produce a daughter, Cassandra, as well as a film crucial to his development as an artist. More on that later.

For the next few years, in partnership with Ivan Reitman and Cinépix, the director pursued funding for his first commercial feature. A Crown corporation, the Canadian Film Development Corporation, put up money for *Shivers* (1975). This would be a controversial decision, as Cronenberg's film was deemed quite a bit more shocking than the erotic comedies the public had come to expect from Cinépix.

Shivers provoked questions in the Canadian parliament, debating the value of spending taxpayers' money on disturbing trash. This film about parasite-slugs turning decent citizens into orgy-zombies was surely not in the public interest. Robert Fulford, under the pseudonym Marshall Delaney, demolished *Shivers* in an article for the magazine *Saturday Night*. The headline is clear: 'You should know how bad this film is. After all, you paid for it.' He considered it 'the most repulsive movie I've ever seen'. Other critics gave poor notices, but some defended the film. Cinema Canada called it a contemporary masterpiece of horror. Roger Ebert, in his 1976 review, was sufficiently impressed to praise Cronenberg's 'invention and imagination'. He describes the parasites as looking like 'bloody eggplants with the jitters', which is about right.

Shivers was a huge hit in Ontario and Quebec, though less so in the rest of Canada. It played at the Cannes Film Festival in May 1975 and at the Edinburgh Film Festival in August that year. It won first prize at the Sitges Festival of Horror Films in October 1976.

Despite all of this, the controversy that Fulford's attack on *Shivers* stirred up, made it harder for Cronenberg to fund his next project. The article even got him kicked out of his apartment later on, when his landlady saw it quoted in the *Globe and Mail* alongside news of who would appear in the director's next picture. The CFDC, later Telefilm Canada, would invest in a Cronenberg production again when Cinépix smuggled it in with a multi-film application for funding support.

In *Rabid* (1977), pornographic actress Marilyn Chambers landed her first straight role, about a woman who undergoes experimental plastic surgery after a crash. On emerging from her coma, she has grown a penile proboscis under one of her armpits and is driven to impregnate others with a rage parasite. This is a change from earlier roles; in *Rabid*, Chambers is the one penetrating the men.

Rabid is the project on which Cronenberg met Carolyn Zeifman, a production assistant. She would also work on his next two movies. They married in 1979 and were together until her death in 2017.

The trajectory now appeared set for a stream of horror pictures. However, Cronenberg's next two films turned out very different from what had gone before, and from each other.

Fast Company (1979), once seen as an aberration, now fits well into the director's wider filmography. There's not much subtext here; it really is about the culture of car racing, its B-movie heart in the right place, and some of its themes would become familiar. '*Fast Company* was about my interest in and love for motor racing and, of course, there's my fascination with technology here again', Cronenberg told *Film Freak Central* in 2003.

Also in 1979, *The Brood* came out. Cronenberg has said that this film was his version of *Kramer vs Kramer*. His marriage to Margaret Hindson was breaking down, their daughter the subject of a custody battle, and these traumas inspired *The Brood*. Taking the word 'psychodrama' literally and making its expression physical, here is the tale of a disturbed woman who receives a radical form of therapy, psychoplasmics, which causes her inner demons to manifest in the form of children. *The Brood* is notable as composer Howard Shore's debut on a Cronenberg film.

Scanners (1981) takes the bio-psychic explorations up a level. Landing at the start of the 'video nasties' scare, this is a key film in 1980s body-horror SF, its notoriety deriving from the scene in which one scanner uses ESP to blow the head off another in a battle of minds. *Scanners* marked the end of Cronenberg's early style, his last film before a breakthrough in sophistication began his critical reappraisal as an auteur with a distinctive vision.

In his personal life, he also enjoyed new beginnings. Brandon, his first child with Carolyn, was born in 1980, and their daughter Caitlin came into the world in 1984. Between these births, he made his most radical film to date, followed by his most mainstream.

Videodrome (1983, filmed in 1981) is where Cronenberg refines his themes then pushes them further than before, daring anyone to stop him. Deborah Harry and James Woods shine in a stunning vision of distorted realities that reads like an analogue rehearsal for our digital future.

The director's next venture into new territory was *The Dead Zone* (1983), based on Stephen King's novel about a man whose powers of precognition emerge when he wakes from a coma. Despite having earlier turned down George Lucas, Cronenberg took very well to directing 'other people's material'. *The Dead Zone* was a hit with critics, thanks in part to Christopher Walken's sensitive lead performance.

1983 was a turning point. *Shivers* and *The Brood* had been shown at the Toronto Festival of Festivals in 1979, only to be called reactionary by critic Robin Wood in the Festival's book, *American Nightmare: Essays on the Horror Film*. Four years later, with Piers Handling commissioned to mount the largest programme of Canadian cinema to date, a Cronenberg retrospective formed an essential and major part of what was now the Toronto International Film Festival. The director insisted that they show only his 35mm films, the professional standard, and not his 16mm shorts or his television work. A good move, this positioned him as a serious filmmaker and allowed the breadth of his achievement to be recognised. *Videodrome* was his latest release, and although the festival tried to get *The Dead Zone* for a gala screening, Paramount refused. Complementing the screenings, TIFF published *The Shape of Rage: The Films of David Cronenberg*, edited by Handling. Built around film professor William Beard's academic paper on the director, along with essays by critics, this book was the first to study Cronenberg's cinema.

Given the director's new acceptance in the mainstream, it's perhaps not surprising that Ivan Reitman proposed a comedy as Cronenberg's next film. Now a successful producer and director in L.A., Reitman offered him *The Hitch Hiker's Guide to the Galaxy*. Douglas Adams, creator of the whole sort of general *H2G2* mish-mash, had already spent years in development hell with a movie version, and had described the attempt to get a film made as like 'trying to grill a steak by having a succession of people coming into the room and breathing on it'. It was a sentiment with which, at one time or another, David Cronenberg would surely have agreed. His movie of Arthur Dent's progress through space-time could have been remarkable, especially his take on the Babel fish, a living creature that you insert into your ear so that you can understand alien languages. It sounds like a Berlitz edition of the game pod from *eXistenZ*.

The infinite improbability of Cronenberg's *Hitch Hiker's Guide* collapsed to zero, but another film had begun to hatch.

When producer Stuart Cornfeld brought a remake of *The Fly* to Brooksfilms, Cronenberg was their preferred director. The first time, he was unavailable, signed up to develop what would become *Total Recall*. Brooks and Cornfeld reluctantly moved on. Then, after many drafts of the PKD adaptation, Cronenberg left the project, which became a tantalising 'what if' in his ghost catalogue. Now that he was free, Brooksfilms asked him again to direct *The Fly* and he agreed on condition that he write the script. It was a match made in insect heaven. Denise Cronenberg joined the production as costume designer; she would work on eight of his features and one short. This was also his last film with cinematographer Mark Irwin.

The Fly was a critical and commercial success and Cronenberg became a bankable director. With talk of a sequel, Mel Brooks wanted more of the same, but that didn't interest Cronenberg. As for his new, mainstream audience? Even *The Fly* could not have prepared them for what came next.

Cronenberg co-wrote *Dead Ringers* (1988) with his friend Norman Snider, who had acted in *Crimes of the Future* and written one of the director's television projects. Nominally based on a book inspired by a real-life case, *Dead Ringers* is a chilling study of co-dependent people on a spiral of self-destruction. Its tale of twin gynaecologists and the actress whose affections they share, used a new kind of split-screen technique that allowed Jeremy Irons to play both twins. Technically innovative, the film is glorious to look at. Peter Suschitzky, Cronenberg's new director of photography, brought a coolly delicate aesthetic, helping to cement the director's reputation as a considerable stylist. Creatively, Cronenberg was on a hot streak. So, where to next? Interzone, for a spot of lunch. *Naked Lunch* (1991).

The 'naked lunch' is defined as the moment when you see 'exactly what's on the end of your fork'. David Cronenberg, always an admirer of William S.

Burroughs's novel, now tried to see what was on the end of his. Was it possible to turn this book into a film? The answer he came to was no, a conclusion that freed him from having to make linear sense of the text. Besides, there is never a film *of* a book, only *from* a book. Cronenberg remarked at the time that to make a straight adaptation would 'cost $400,000,000 and be banned in every country in the world'. Instead, he made a film that blended incidents from the author's life with episodes from his literary works.

Naked Lunch was an artistic triumph and won several awards. One of the great films about writing, it is a metatextual commentary on the novel's own creation, as well as on the suffering that artists often inflict on the civilians who love them. Some critics were turned off by the film, but many found it compelling. It wasn't a hit at the box office, and perhaps it's not a surprise that this disturbing, tragic, hilarious, hallucinatory, drugged-up, bugged-out, psychedelic fairground of death and grief, with its Mugwump jism and talking-asshole-typewriters, put some cinemagoers off.

Such a divided response may have placed the artist in his comfort zone, so it was time to step out of it. Few may have expected him to adapt a Broadway hit, though the one he chose was not exactly *The Lion King*. A love story, spy thriller and meditation on identity and colonialism, *M. Butterfly* (1993) was his first film since *Fast Company* not to feature horror or science fiction. Reteaming the director with Jeremy Irons, the film is a different sort of tragedy. David Henry Hwang adapted it from his own play, itself inspired by Puccini and the true story of a French diplomat's compromising affair with a Chinese singer, as well as other literary antecedents. The writer would work with Cronenberg again on Howard Shore's opera of *The Fly*.

After *M. Butterfly*'s lack of success, it was time to get extreme again with another impossible movie from another unfilmable book.

Crash (1996) is an erotic tale of everyday sociopaths, involving motor accidents as the stimuli for emotional responses. It takes the term 'car porn' at face value and turns it into art, just like J. G. Ballard had done a generation before. Cronenberg's film updates the setting to contemporary Toronto, but the soul of the author haunts the city's motorways. According to one early viewer in the UK, the film was 'like *Casualty* with full-frontal sex'.

It would be three years before Cronenberg released his next film, *eXistenZ* (1999). His first movie since *Videodrome* not based on another source, this was his return to a world both familiar and strange. The idea for the story came from his 1995 *Shift* magazine interview with Salman Rushdie, who at the time lived under a *fatwa* issued by religious extremists for having written a novel, *The Satanic Verses*. With his interest in computer games, Cronenberg asked himself what if a designer of virtual-reality games were faced with a similar threat. *eXistenZ* revived his old style of body horror for an entertaining romp through a kind of pastoral cyberspace in which the human body is only one component in the machine.

In hindsight, *eXistenZ* seems like the filmmaker's equivalent of a rock star retiring the old hits by touring them one last time, blowing the minds of the faithful before taking up novel-writing, or indeed trout farming.

In 2000, Cronenberg made another short film. The six-minute *Camera*, a moving meditation on the nature of utility and loss, was commissioned along with other shorts to celebrate the 25th anniversary of the Toronto International Film Festival. *Camera* features his fourth collaboration with Leslie Carlson, after *Videodrome*, *The Dead Zone* and *The Fly*.

If *eXistenZ* was an amusement, his next feature, *Spider* (2002), was all psychological depth, some of it terrifying. A sensitive and troubling adaptation of Patrick McGrath's fine second novel, *Spider* shows us the world of a schizophrenic man moving between his shifting perceptions of reality. Director, writer and lead actors all deferred their salaries to get this film made. The result is one of Cronenberg's greatest films, with Ralph Fiennes giving a perfect, detailed performance in the lead, and Miranda Richardson extraordinary in multiple roles. *Spider* marked the start of a new phase of literary adaptations that would take Cronenberg from McGrath to DeLillo and beyond, by way of comic books and a biography.

Partly because he'd lost his shirt on *Spider*, Cronenberg signed on to direct *A History of Violence* (2005). True, he needed a payday, but he made commercial necessity into a virtue, entering new territory yet again. In 1997, John Wagner, creator of Judge Dredd, had published the source comic, illustrated by Vince Locke. Starring Viggo Mortensen, this was a noirish story of a man fleeing his past but always preparing for the day when it might catch up with him. Cronenberg's film examines what happens when violence tears through a family and a community. It resonated then, as it does today, with an America torn apart by frequent mass shootings. *A History of Violence* was a critically lauded triumph as well as Cronenberg's biggest hit in years.

Another project he completed in 2005 was the art-book, *Red Cars*, derived from a film he had tried to make some years earlier, as far back as 1986. This limited-edition book included the screenplay for a potential movie about the rivalry between two Ferrari drivers in the 1961 Formula One championship.

Cronenberg worked again with Viggo Mortensen on *Eastern Promises* (2007), also starring Naomi Watts, who plays a midwife drawn into the underworld by her discovery of a diary. The script was by Steven Knight, who had written *Dirty Pretty Things* (2002). A tense thriller grounded in a power struggle within the Russian mafia in London, this was another critical favourite, a hit at the box office, and an Oscar-winner for Mortensen. It continued Cronenberg's new direction of making more conventional pictures that carried his DNA, fulfilling, at last, his early desire to 'sell out' but without compromising.

In 2007, Cronenberg also directed a three-minute short about a Jewish man, played by himself, threatening to commit suicide live on television as he waits in the last cinema on Earth. Meanwhile, commentators discuss both Jewishness and cinema. *At the Suicide of the Last Jew in the World in the Last Cinema in the World* was commissioned as part of a portmanteau film to celebrate the Cannes Film Festival. It is both a personal statement and a typically wry answer to the brief.

2008 was busy. The exhibition *Chromosomes* opened at the Rome Film Festival, and Howard Shore's opera of *The Fly* premiered in Paris in July with a libretto by David Henry Hwang and costumes by Denise Cronenberg. Conducted by Plácido Domingo, the opera was directed by Cronenberg himself. After it landed in Los Angeles, the *L.A. Times* called it 'a monster smash'. Other critics were less than kind.

This was not the only time that Cronenberg had considered a new version of *The Fly*. He mentioned in a 2011 *Rue Morgue* interview that he had an idea for a film 'lateral' to his original, one that wouldn't be a sequel. As he then elaborated to *Empire* in 2012, it would be 'a meditation on flyness'. That film is yet to be made.

Following the opera, for both director and composer, it was back to the movies and back in time, to the origin of psychoanalysis.

If Cronenberg ever made a Merchant Ivory picture, it might look something like *A Dangerous Method* (2011). Adapted by Christopher Hampton from his play, the film dissected the power dynamics between Freud, Jung and their protégé Sabina Spielrein. A strong cast, Keira Knightley, Viggo Mortensen, Michael Fassbender and Sarah Gadon, acquitted themselves very well. This was on the face of it an unusual piece for the director, but again, one of its themes is familiar: the effect of psychological states on the physical wellbeing of an individual. *A Dangerous Method* won several awards and was a moderate financial success.

Rebounding again from the mainstream, he chose another allegedly unfilmable novel as his next project. *Cosmopolis* (2012), from the book by Don DeLillo, is an experiment in form as well as a showcase for the talent of Robert Pattinson, here taking the lead as Packer, a financial wizard who loses millions on the stock market as he takes a slow limousine ride across town to get a haircut.

David Cronenberg took *Cosmopolis* to Cannes, where it was nominated for the Palme d'Or. His son Brandon joined him there, as his debut movie *Antiviral* was set to open in the *Un Certain Regard* section. The Cronenbergs were the first father and son pair to bring their movies to Cannes in the same year. In a public Q&A, TIFF's artistic director Cameron Bailey discussed their films and careers with the two directors. When asked about his father's influence, Brandon said, 'I don't have enough distance from his work to be influenced by it in the way that I think people usually mean', but he added, 'He's my father, so I think I've been influenced by him that way: we share genes, I grew up around him, we have a very good relationship.' David praised his son's film, saying that seeing him on the red carpet was emotional. 'Because, as I said to Bran, it took me twenty years to get to Cannes. And here he is with his first film. But it was really terrific because I had seen the movie and I knew it was a terrific film, so I was very excited for him.'

2013 brought a major retrospective at TIFF. *David Cronenberg: Evolution*, a showcase of props and artefacts from his films, formed part of the *Cronenberg Project*, celebrating his work with new 35mm prints of the restored films. The Museum of Contemporary Canadian Art commissioned six artists to produce works inspired by the director. In the same year, his nineteenth professional film got the green light.

Maps to the Stars (2014) written by Bruce Wagner, had something of an arrested development. Wagner had composed a screenplay years before, but when the project stalled, he used some of its ideas in his acidly funny novel, *Dead Stars*. When the film reignited in 2013, Wagner was still on board. Appropriately, Cronenberg and his team shot this transgressive Hollywood satire in Los Angeles.

Around this time he made a short, *The Nest*, commissioned by the EYE festival and released on YouTube. It acted as a trailer for his novel *Consumed*, which he published in 2014. Immediately recognised as serious literature, the book translated its author's obsessions into a new medium. Stephen King called it 'an eye-opening dazzler'. Cronenberg the artist had mutated.

The next year, he and Carolyn became grandparents with the birth of Caitlin's son.

While promoting *Captain Fantastic* in 2016, Viggo Mortensen suggested to *Variety* that Cronenberg, having spent years trying to chase finance for his films, might be on the point of retiring from the cinema in favour of writing novels. Mortensen praised his sometime director as one of the greats. 'I can't think of another around that long that stays as fresh', he said. 'It's ridiculous... Here's one of our greatest directors and he has so much trouble getting his movies made.'

On 19 June 2017, Carolyn Cronenberg died. After marrying David in 1979, she retired from her film career to raise their children. She later directed and edited documentaries including two about *A History of Violence* and its journey to Cannes.

In the year of his bereavement, and despite difficulties with getting financing, Cronenberg kept busy. He set up a miniseries adaptation of *Consumed* at AMC in 2017, which fell apart despite its writing team having progressed quite far. The project, one he intended not to write, headed for Netflix but they too passed on it. In the new world of CGI franchises owned by Disney, *weird* was neither profitable nor desirable.

In interviews, the director discussed a possible end to his film career. 'If this is it for the so-called Cronenberg canon, then so be it. You can't worry about legacy', he told the *Globe and Mail* in 2019.

Whatever about his work behind the camera, he didn't entirely say goodbye to cinema but took up acting again, a side profession that he'd pursued for decades, essaying parts that interested him and helped pay the bills. In a 2020

Hollywood Reporter interview, he said that he was enjoying acting in Albert Shin's *Disappearance at Clifton Hill*. 'Even though I thought I was finished with film, I miss the set and the people you work with.'

This director has sometimes discussed the idea that cinema as we knew it is over, that streaming and other media are the future, and that he is not sentimental about the demise of movies. At the time of this writing, the TV series of *Consumed* is looking for a new home with its creator once again attached to write and direct. As his adaptations of other people's material have always been transformative, it would be interesting to see how, in the new web-televisual environment, David Cronenberg adapts himself.

The Body Horror Picture Show

If there is one subgenre that requires the opposite of social distancing, it's body horror. As style and subject, it is central to the first phase of David Cronenberg's feature film career. Witness the orgiastic parasites in *Shivers*, the vampiric proboscis in *Rabid*, the psychic offspring in *The Brood*; or the explosions in *Scanners*, the penetrations in *Videodrome*, the fusions in *The Fly*. Body horror recurs with various degrees of potency in the later films, even *A Dangerous Method*, if you count spanking. We know only too well that body horror also exists in real life. In February 2020, while promoting *Disappearance at Clifton Hill*, Cronenberg told *The Hollywood Reporter* that in scientific terms the coronavirus is 'just business as usual on planet Earth', allowing that 'socially, it's scary'. This observation is not only astute; it chimes with the dynamic in many of his films, especially the early, gory ones.

Despite having made films about fictional outbreaks, he is not a prophet of pandemics. Nor is he alone in understanding how, as our destruction of the planet goes unchecked, parasites take advantage of the opportunities we hold open to them. But he does have an original perspective: as an artist, he is on the side of the virus. From the parasite's perspective, contagion makes the world a better place. It also sets us free from the repression imposed by society. Everybody wins.

The director has said that his films should be seen 'from the point of view of the disease'; he identifies with the characters after they have become infected. He shows us how fragile we are, how our societies are constructs which exist by consensus. Interviewed by Bette Gordon for *BOMB* magazine in 1989, he said that '…because of our necessity to impose our own structure of perception on things, we look on ourselves as being relatively stable. But, in fact, when I look at a person I see this maelstrom of organic, chemical and electron chaos; volatility and instability, shimmering; and the ability to change and transform and transmute'.

Cronenberg has discussed human DNA in viral terms, as in Dawkins' 'selfish gene', positing that the body is principally a vehicle for transmitting our genetic material. In this respect, our purpose is no different from that of a housefly, or HIV, the drive to reproduce being central to all organisms. We all come from the same ancestor, far back in our evolutionary past, which makes us distantly related to viruses. Unlike other relatives, we usually invite this one in. Then, despite the late Bill Hicks's assertion that a human is 'a virus with shoes', we learn that we're also the shoes the virus wears.

The literary origin of body horror could be traced to Mary Shelley, with her creature built from the parts of fresh cadavers and a soul sparked by lightning, Doctor Frankenstein being a serial killer in reverse. But there are other plausible sources. Cronenberg, brought up in a liberal Jewish household, may have encountered the story of the golem, a clay homunculus given life by use of a name inscribed on its forehead. Like Frankenstein's creature, the golem wreaks havoc when it escapes the control of those who suffered it to live. Gustav Meyrink's novel *The Golem* makes an interesting companion to Shelley's *Frankenstein*.

There is a case to be made that the genre began earlier still, with the tale of a man who engineers the mortification of his own body so that he might transcend the world of flesh. Sounds like *Videodrome*? Not exactly. Golgotha is the most successful viral campaign in history and is also one of the first fantasies of transhumanism. Mel Gibson's film adaptation, *The Passion of the Christ*, is bloody, lacerating, and realistic in its sadism. Unsurprisingly, it is venerated by the sort of people who would, without needing to have seen it, ban *Crash* as depraved. If they watched Cronenberg's films, they might notice a familiar theme: a kind of anti-transubstantiation. Max Renn's 'new flesh', the agony of the Mantles, the scarification of Vaughan: these are a few examples. And what is Vaughan, *Crash*'s 'hoodlum scientist', if not a Christ figure? Even as an atheist, one may still appreciate such imagery, which carries within it the potency of myth.

Cronenberg's own variety of body horror emerged in the wake of George A. Romero's political allegory, *Night of the Living Dead*. *Shivers* further developed the genre's potential to be more than just bloody disgusting. It had a philosophy. As Katrina Onstad wrote in a 2013 article for *Toronto Life*: 'For Cronenberg, amateur biologist and professional existentialist, everything starts with the body. Over and over, his stories show how the body cannot be denied; to suppress base urges and functions is to invite chaos, madness'.

That philosophy is as crucial to his films as effects and prosthetics. The transformations in Cronenberg's cinema arise directly out of the characters' predicament. They are a form of psychogenic fugue made flesh. Brundlefly, though his transition breaks Ronnie's heart, is increasingly curious, and looks forward to becoming the first 'insect politician'. Equally, the Mantle twins realise that they must modify their physical form to find freedom, even maturity. If we think of them as possessing *two bodies, two minds, one soul,* the singular use of *form* is appropriate. Something radical is required: separation.

Just as body horror often involves a destructive-creative physical expression of psychological states (*The Brood, Scanners, Videodrome*), it can also take the form of erotic disfigurement (*Crash*); symbiosis or mutation (*Shivers, The Fly, Naked Lunch* and others). It can involve the use of technology and drugs to release a person's identity through death (*Dead Ringers*). In *eXistenZ*, biotechnology can free our minds from physical reality itself.

Throughout the 1970s and 1980s, as he refined his art and skill with each successive film, other directors made their own explorations in parallel. David Lynch's 1977 debut, *Eraserhead*, recalled the surrealism of Buñuel; as did some of Cronenberg's own imagery. In 1979, Dan O'Bannon's concept for the Alien's reproductive cycle (as distinct from the designs by H. R. Giger) appeared to borrow from *Shivers* as much as from, say, the wood wasp. In 1982, John Carpenter unleashed *The Thing* and John Landis gave us *An*

American Werewolf in London, both of which amazed audiences with their creature effects. That year, Cronenberg worked with Landis' werewolf-wrangler, Rick Baker, on *Videodrome*. A few years on, while Brundlefly was emerging, Stuart Gordon made *Re-Animator* (1985) from the works of H. P. Lovecraft. Bryan Yuzna's classic *Society* (1990) is a smart and sly satire, which echoes some of Cronenberg's ideas about family dynamics. The outrageous plasticity that *Elm Street* veteran Screaming Mad George (a.k.a. Joji Tani) brought to the effects in Yuzna's film, reminds us of *Videodrome*, though its true antecedent is *The Thing*. In the years before rampant CGI, the physical props and effects designed and built for these movies, represented the pinnacle of the art. Those handmade, workshop-tooled objects took visceral hold on the viewer's imagination and never let go.

A couple of years before *Society*, Cronenberg made *Dead Ringers*. Here the exploration of flesh is ever-present, in 'mutant' gynaecology, drug-induced hallucinations, and the suggestion that being born a twin is a form of body modification by means of genetics. The implied horror of the gynaecological surgical instruments in *Dead Ringers* turns into actual, queasy terror when they are used by a doctor strung out on medication, as indeed they would be if used by anyone, stoned or not. More than one woman, having seen this film, has vowed never to watch it again, and its power to disturb remains undiminished.

Cronenberg's next three films offered much to alarm the sensitive. The improbable creatures of *Naked Lunch* gave it an *ick* factor that was intentionally funny, as with the talking-asshole-typewriter. You didn't get that in a Bruckheimer movie. The quieter madness of *M. Butterfly* followed this, a film in which someone's identity is changed by means of a prosthetic we can all wear: the lover's self-delusion. Before it became a film, J. G. Ballard's *Crash* had already been controversial, to say the least. The director updated the story while preserving its essence, celebrating the cult of the arousing car accident. As with Ballard, for Cronenberg the collision of desire and chrome, Lincoln and libido, is 'a fertilising rather than a destructive event'. The body horror in *Crash* is not caused by parasites but by humans themselves. Who can forget Rosanna Arquette's vulvic leg wound? It's erotic *haute couture* in stitches.

eXistenZ was officially his first non-adapted screenplay since *Videodrome*, to which it serves as a companion piece. This psychedelic fairground ride revisits his purest themes: the nature of reality, the limits of perception, the fragility of body and mind. It also bursts with beautiful bio-ware: the ports and umbys, the pods, the gristle-guns. In *eXistenZ*, with commendable but rare realism, to install the modification can really hurt.

Spider may not seem like a body horror story, but given that a mind is the product of a nervous system, it counts. Here, the horror is internalised, in a drama that investigates the ideas of *eXistenZ* with a different method. Focusing on Dennis Cleg's struggle with reality, *Spider* challenges our perception of ourselves and of other people. In some mental illnesses, this can shift catastrophically, without warning or awareness. Cleg's voices may very well be more resonant to us now than in 2002, because in today's world of connected isolation, our panopticon of telepresence, we have voices in our heads all the time, getting us to buy things while allowing us to present multiple personalities to the world. Cronenberg has spoken about this in interviews, and it makes ever more sense now that the membranes between individual identities are in flux. 'Who do you think you are?' is a question no one can now answer with absolute certainty. A human mind and body can be viewed as an integrated backup disk for the program that we are all running. Mental illness is not what happens when the disk becomes corrupted; it's a reasonable response (as Ballard suggested) to the world in which we live. It's the new body horror, wreaking changes as important as those induced by the parasites in Cronenberg's movies.

The idea that we are merging with our machines suggests that the natural endpoint of body modification is transhumanism. In a post-human society, the moneyed classes may choose to merge their flesh with the internet, and others may have the choice made for them. But who will feed the cat? The rest of us, probably, an underclass that finds work servicing what remains of the virtual rich.

In a world where these biomechanical hybrids are the audience, the makers of stories will have a problem. If reality can no longer exist objectively, whither fiction? All those scriptwriters teaching film workshops will be out of a job. The Cathode Ray Mission will have won: television, or its successor, will become indistinguishable from reality.

In the future, should those post-humans watch one of Cronenberg's films, we can imagine what they will make of that nice romantic comedy *Shivers*. To our future alien selves, *Videodrome* will be an instruction manual, and *Naked Lunch* might just be *cinema verité*.

The last word, for now, belongs to David Cronenberg himself. Interviewed by *The Daily Beast*, he said, 'I consider myself an existentialist and an atheist, and I think that body is what we are. That's not diminishing it to me; it's just accepting the reality of it. So, if the human body is the first fact of human existence, then immediately you see why I focus on the body.'

Early Short Films

Transfer (1966)

Producer, writer, cinematographer, editor and director: David Cronenberg. With: Richard Osolen (editing), Margaret Hindson (sound), Stephen Nosko (co-producer and sound). Canada, Colour, 16mm. Running time: 6 minutes, 27 seconds.
Cast: Rafe McPherson, Mort Ritts.

Story

Ralph, a patient, has followed his psychiatrist into the snow-covered wilderness, to protest that he loves him. Seeing that the feeling is unrequited, the patient tries to get the attention of the doctor, who is disturbed by his arrival.

The short begins with the doctor pouring grape juice, then squeezing toothpaste onto a brush, which he stirs in the juice before brushing his teeth. He's dressed for winter in a long coat with a scarf and a hat, but he's wearing sunglasses. A voice from behind: his patient, Ralph, is there. 'How did you find me?' the doctor asks. 'The others gave up long ago.'

What kind of doctor is this? More to the point, what kind of patients did he have, that drove him to escape into a wilderness 'hundreds of miles from civilization'? Ralph may be a clue. He's in love with the doctor, who himself doesn't seem terribly stable. From their discussion, it seems that the doctor didn't treat his patients quite as effectively as he might have. Now he sits in a chair and analyses Ralph again as the patient lies down in the snow.

Comment

There's a joke about a lab rat that has trained the scientist to feed it whenever it rings a bell. *Transfer*, David Cronenberg's first film, is an absurdist take on that story. The performances are over the top, which may have been the intention, adding to the absurdity of what amounts to a surreal sketch. On the other hand, the film's theatrical sensibility could be a function of inexperience, this being a student production. Over a minute of the running time comprises titles stencilled by the director. As a first film, *Transfer* is promising, but few contemporary viewers might have guessed how Cronenberg would fulfil that promise.

From the Drain (1967)

Production: Emergent Films. Produced by Stephen Nosko and Mort Ritts. Sound by Margaret Hindson. Writer, director, cinematographer, editor: David Cronenberg. Running time: 14 minutes.
Cast: Stephen Nosko, Mort Ritts.

Story

The film takes place in a bathroom at the Disabled War Veterans' Recreation Centre. Two men sit in the bath, the first at the far end from the tap. He is worried that something will come out of the drain. He discusses his experiences during the war and says that he knows how such creatures might be created. The second man encourages him to swap places and to look in the drain to reassure himself. When tendrils come out of the drain and strangle the first man, the second takes out a notebook and pen and starts writing. Dark liquid spills out of the first man's mouth. The second takes up the first man's shoes and puts them in a closet with a pile of other shoes. He picks a pair of shoes for himself and leaves the bathroom.

Comment

Cronenberg's second film is something of a comedy sketch: part-Pinter, part-Python. There's even a hint of Beckett. The performances are idiosyncratic, in keeping with the ideas conveyed. In the year that George Lucas made *THX-1138 4EB* and Scorsese filmed *The Big Shave*, *From the Drain* also introduces concepts that would surface again in its director's career. The threat coming from the drain would return in *Shivers*, with a proper horror star as its target.

Early Feature Films

Stereo (1969)
a.k.a Stereo (Tile 3B of a CAEE Educational Mosaic) (1969)
Production company: Emergent Films
Writer, director, cinematographer, editor: David Cronenberg
Canada release: 23 June 1969 (National Arts Centre)
US release: 30 November 1973 (NYC)
Running time: 65 minutes
Budget $3,500
Cast: Ron Mlodzik, Iain Ewing, Clara Mayer, Jack Messinger, Paul Mulholland.

Story
A silent world of the near future. In a modern campus that appears deserted, a helicopter touches down and a man gets out. Mysterious in his black cloak, looking like a stage magician, he searches for an entrance to the facility. A voice-over informs us that this man is one of eight subjects who willingly submitted to 'pattern brain surgery' as a result of which their telepathic ability has been activated. They do not need to speak, as they can communicate directly with each other via the power of the mind. The telepaths are preparing for their first meeting with all eight present as a group. Doctor Luther Stringfellow – an aphrodisiast who deals in the 'sociochemistry of the erotic' and who created this experiment – is not present. Is he watching from afar?

At various sites across the campus, the subjects walk around, or run through the corridors, or perambulate in the gardens, and if they greet each other, they do so without speaking. Researchers study the subjects, each for a different response. The subjects have formed 'psychic addictions' to the researchers and get emotionally disturbed if they're parted from them for too long.

Meanwhile, the telepaths work with each other. In one area, a mostly naked man takes off a woman's top and while she sits blindfolded, he strokes an anatomical model of a torso, its innards on display. Elsewhere, two other subjects study Tarot cards as all around the building, telepaths go about performing tasks.

The voice-over discusses the need for dominant telepathic minds to surrender to the group, which will in the future overtake the nuclear family, now a redundant unit. Some telepaths, wishing to avoid contact with others, project a false identity that disturbs the communicant with images of depravity.

Now there is a scene of group sex, shown in slow-motion as the voice-over tells us that the subjects have resisted sharing their minds telepathically, even though EEG scans had shown their connection. By now, two of the subjects have committed suicide. Doctor Stringfellow may have chosen to stay away because the psychic dependency between subject and researcher could be mutual and too dangerous. At the end of the film, the narrator reveals that the data on the six surviving subjects will take some time to understand. The experiment is incomplete.

Comment

For a long time, David Cronenberg's early films were not readily available. It's tempting to wonder what a viewer of *Rabid* in the 1970s or *Scanners* in the 1980s might have made of *Stereo*. An art film, it has more in common with the European New Wave than Hollywood. Visually influenced by the works of Alain Resnais (*Last Year in Marienbad*), *Stereo* reminds us too of the literary New Wave that was then remaking the idea of science fiction. It fits with the works of such pioneers as Ballard, Aldiss, Priest and Moorcock, turning their gazes away from outer space and towards inner space. *Stereo*'s subject matter and style are reminiscent of these authors' experiments in psycho-erotics, as well as their tropes of a post-disaster world in which renegade scientists transgress the norms of straight society. Ron Mlodzik's unnamed character comes across as a possible avatar of Moorcock's Eternal Champion. Mlodzik's presence adds a creatively decadent flavour to *Stereo* and helps inform its omnisexual aesthetic. Early Kubrick comes to mind also: the film is beautiful to look at, its black-and-white photography crisp and luminous, elegantly juxtaposing the austere angularity of the University of Toronto campus with the building's pastoral surroundings. This gives us a sense of a larger world which seems to exist somehow next door to other Cronenberg films in which the most extreme scientific pursuits take place in verdant settings. The eeriness of *Stereo*'s world is born partly out of necessity. The director had no budget for sound sync, so he made a silent film, adding a voice-over later. He shot his cast posing and staging sequences on location and completed the story in the edit. Clarity comes where the voice-over and the visuals intersect and the film purports to be an educational document. A fly-on-the-wall approach to the surreal helps the film transcend its limited resources. *Stereo* was ahead of its time, but who, fifty years on, might its audience be? Fans, certainly, completing their experience. But *Stereo* has more than curiosity value and is probably best seen in a double-bill with its successor, *Crimes of the Future*. These films fire the starting gun. *Stereo* predicts *Scanners* as both films feature characters gaining psychic abilities through drilling holes in their heads. In stark contrast with other counter-cultural films of the time, this is no *Easy Rider*. Given its duration and its themes, *Stereo* could have worked as an episode of *The Outer Limits* but might have been too weird and undramatic. Cronenberg, 26 when he shot this film, was finding his feet and playing with ideas. Those ideas are bold for the time, but a viewer today will appreciate just how much bolder his cinema became. *Stereo* marks the beginning of what some have called the 'Cronenverse'. His next film would expand on the experimental vocabulary established here, and discover its limits.

Crimes of the Future (1970)

Production company: Emergent Films.
Writer, director, cinematographer, editor: David Cronenberg
Australia release: June 1970

US release: 10 August 1984
Running time: 63 minutes
Budget $20,000
Cast: Jon Lidolt, Jack Messinger, Ronald Mlodzik, Paul Mulholland, Tania Zolty.

Story

The year is 1997. Adrian Tripod, pronounced Tri-POD, is the director of a
dermatology clinic called the House of Skin. He's on the hunt for his old
mentor, the insane dermatologist Antoine Rouge, who has disappeared. The
world has been turned upside down by a bizarre pandemic, Rouge's Malady,
caused by the use of cosmetic products. This virulent outbreak has killed all
women who have reached puberty, and the only females left on the planet are
young girls. Some of Tripod's patients have their fingernails painted red to be
more feminine. Watching their inexplicable activities, and the strange foamy
liquid some of them exude from their bodies, Tripod knows that the inmates
have taken over the asylum, and it is time for him to leave.

Tripod steps into the barren world outside, hoping to find Rouge. On his
journey, he encounters a series of strange institutions, and men trying to
come to terms with the new world order. At the Institute of Neo-Venereal
Disease, Tripod meets a man who grows organs inside his body and has them
continually removed before he grows more. The man considers this parody
of reproduction to be a form of 'creative cancer', and he becomes sad when
the organs are taken away. At the Oceanic Podiatry Group, Tripod performs
'foot therapy' on men whose legs end in various types of appendage: flippers,
webbed feet, tentacles. It is at the Gynaecological Research Foundation that
Tripod discovers both horror and hope. This is a group of heterosexual
paedophiles, who follow their leader, Tiomkin. The Foundation has 'imported'
and is keeping captive a very young girl, who has had puberty induced
prematurely. Stealing a gun from the Foundation's security guard, Tripod
chases some of the men away but they take the girl with them as they leave
the building. Later, in a hotel where Rouge was reputed to have stayed, Tripod
takes rooms for himself and his fellow subversives from the Foundation. He
meets the concierge, who exhibits a rootlike growth from one of his nostrils
and believes it to be an extension of his nerve cells, perhaps an antenna.
Tripod asks him about Rouge, but he doesn't answer.

Now Tripod sits in the hotel with the men he had chased. They all agree that
there must be no delay in impregnating the girl, their 'strange, unfathomable
captive', before she falls prey to Rouge's Malady. After one of the men fails
to perform this task, Tripod enters the room where the girl is being kept.
Sensing the presence of Adrian Rouge, Tripod sees that the girl has some of the
white foam on her finger. She puts it in her mouth, as if it were cream. Tripod
reaches over to her and comes away with the white foam on his own finger.
He lies back in a chair and cries black tears. The girl, who is Antoine Rouge
reincarnated, watches him inscrutably.

Comment

Thanks to a literature grant with which he intended to write a novel, David Cronenberg made a film. *Crimes of the Future*, stylistically and thematically a companion to *Stereo*, was the last stop before his professional career began, and is a more openly satirical film with an emphasis on black humour. Once again Ron Mlodzik gives an ethereal performance, as Adrian Tripod, one of the director's renegade scientists.

This film, if made today, would be highly problematic, with its excision of all adult women, and the suggestion that the solution to the apocalypse is to impregnate a young girl whose puberty has been induced early. There's madness to its implications, yet Kim Newman has dismissed the director's first two features as showing that it's possible for a film to be interesting and boring at the same time. *Crimes of the Future* delineates what might happen if the free love of the 1960s met a dystopian catastrophe. Although the 'men without women' theme is not new, Cronenberg gives it a horrific twist. One may ask how the bodies were disposed of and what enormous grief marked the beginning of this desolate new society.

Some of these ideas will return even stranger. The organs grown and removed from the body foretell Nola Carveth's reproductive procedure in *The Brood*. Amusingly named institutions and groups will become a staple of the director's work.

Although similar in form to *Stereo*, this picture exhibits notable differences. It's shot in colour, the contrast making it seem half of a diptych with the first film. It's also filmed in silence with the soundtrack added later. Here there's more than just narration: strange animal noises and electronic effects add to the tainted atmosphere. We see the young filmmaker's heady confidence of not knowing what can't be done, yet this short movie still feels more literary than cinematic, fitting in with the SF New Wave.

Jon Lidolt, a film worker at distribution house Filmcanada, became a friend of the director, having seen and liked parts of *Stereo*. Lidolt, who acts in *Crimes of the Future* as well as designing its titles, spoke to *DVD Savant* in 2007 about his experience, which was wholly positive. He likened the shoot to making a silent film, about which he learned from having met Lillian Gish. Without a soundtrack, more flexibility was possible: if you had to reshoot, you could do so without invalidating the footage already taken.

Cronenberg had started filming in black-and-white, but thanks to the arts grant, he could now afford to shoot in colour if he used a ratio of less than 2:1. Starting over, he had enough money for production – camera, colour stock, lab facilities – but not for shooting sound, or hiring actors. So he called on friends, including Lidolt, for whom this appears to have been his only role as an actor. As with *Stereo*, Cronenberg shot this second feature on the University of Toronto campus, in what would now be called guerilla style, i.e., without permission. Lidolt said that there wasn't really a script, just notes that Cronenberg consulted, but without dialogue, a traditional script wasn't required. Besides, the director knew what he wanted, shooting handheld with a rented Arriflex: the only tripod on the picture was Adrian.

After these two underground features, Cronenberg realised that he had done what he could in the form, and he needed to make a living, so his plan was to go commercial. The question was, in then-conservative Canada, whether anyone would want to buy what he was selling.

Shivers (1975)

Produced by John Dunning, André Link, Alfred Pariser and Ivan Reitman
Cinematographer: Robert Saad
Sound: Michael Higgs, Dan Goldberg
Music Supervisor: Ivan Reitman
Special make-up and creature effects: Joe Blasco
Written and directed by David Cronenberg
Filming dates: 21 August to 17 September 1974
First release: Montreal, 10 October 1975
US release: 6 July 1976
UK release: 13 June 1976
Running time: 87 minutes
Budget: $180,000
Cast: Paul Hampton (Roger St. Luc), Lynn Lowry (Nurse Forsythe), Allan
Migicovsky (Nicholas Tudor), Susan Petrie (Janine Tudor), Joe Silver (Rollo Linsky),
Barbara Steele (Betts)

Background

Orgy of the Blood Parasites. That was the working title of the film that
David Cronenberg hoped would announce his arrival. He brought the script
to John Dunning and André Link of Cinépix, an independent distributor
known for light pornography. As Cinépix's attempts to get funding dragged
on, Cronenberg went to Los Angeles to seek backers. There he spoke with
Roger Corman, who expressed an interest. The director also met Jonathan
Demme, who told him that Cinépix had been shopping the script around.
This was news to Cronenberg, who returned to Canada to confront them but
by the time he arrived, Cinépix had finally got money from the Canadian Film
Development Corporation. After three years of trying, *Shivers* was ready to go
and would be produced by Cronenberg's friend Ivan Reitman.

   With a fifteen-day schedule, *Shivers* started rolling at Île des Sœurs (Nuns'
Island) on the Saint Lawrence River, Montréal. The setting for Starliner Towers
was a hotel on the island. Cronenberg lived nearby; the infamous bath scene
with Betts and the parasite was shot in his apartment.

   As Betts, Cronenberg cast horror queen Barbara Steele, noted for Mario
Bava's *Black Sunday* (1960) and Roger Corman's *The Pit and the Pendulum*
(1961), among others.

   The creatures and special effects were devised by Joe Blasco, often credited
as the first to create bladder effects such as the parasite moving under skin.

   Both hirings gave the film a good start, but there were misunderstandings.
When Cronenberg slapped Sue Petrie (playing Janine), Barbara Steele
threatened to punch him. However, Petrie had requested the slap to help her
cry for a scene, after using an onion had not worked, and she had rehearsed it
with the director.

   While *Shivers* was being shot in a few rooms on a small budget, *The Towering*

Inferno was busting blocks around the world. The two movies couldn't have been more different, which illustrated how far Cronenberg was from the mainstream. For the general public, horror meant *The Exorcist*, *Jaws* and Hammer films.

Shivers didn't have an easy path with the critics, some of whom reviewed it as though they were protecting Canada from an assault on its morals. Robert Fulford in his *Saturday Night* article called the film 'a disgrace to everyone connected with it, including the taxpayers'. Having provoked the infamous debate in parliament, Cronenberg must have been pleased when *Shivers* became one of only a few CFDC-funded films to return the government's investment, earning $5,000,000 at the box office, the most profitable Canadian film to date.

Story

A commercial slideshow promotes the benefits of Starliner Towers, a new luxury high-rise complex built on an island in Montreal. This cuts to the manager, Merrick, welcoming a hip young couple of prospective tenants. Meanwhile, in one of the apartments, Doctor Emil Hobbes strangles a young woman, Annabelle Brown, then cuts open her stomach and pours acid into the wound before killing himself. We then see Nicholas Tudor examine his body in a bathroom mirror as he brushes his teeth; he finds strange convulsions under his abdominal skin. On the way to work, he visits Annabelle's apartment and, reeling from the horrific scene, he flees. Starliner's doctor, Roger St. Luc, finds the bodies and calls the police. Hobbes' medical partner, Rollo Linsky, reveals to St. Luc that he and Hobbes had been working to create a parasite that could take over the function of a human organ. Nick's convulsions get worse, and he leaves work early. Back home, he vomits over his balcony, hitting the umbrella of one of two women walking below. Startled, they think it's a dead bird as it bounces off. But Nick has vomited a parasite, which slithers away unseen, going on to attack other residents. In the basement laundry, the parasite knocks a woman unconscious and attaches itself to her face. In his office, Doctor St. Luc, assisted by Nurse Forsythe, sees an elderly resident complaining of stomach lumps, which the man thinks might be an STD he caught from Annabelle Brown. Nick's wife, Janine, discusses his recent odd behaviour with her friend Betts. When she gets home, she sees Nick unconscious on the floor, having vomited a pool of blood. Nick reassures Janine about his health as outside, some children are scared away by the parasite rolling out of the Tudors' mail slot. Later, alone in bed, Nick speaks lovingly to the lumps in his chest. In her apartment, Betts runs a bath while the radio announces the murder-suicide of Emil Hobbes and Annabelle Brown. Rollo Linsky calls St. Luc from downtown. He has found notes revealing Hobbes's secret plan to combine an aphrodisiac and a venereal disease in the parasite; this could turn the world into a vast orgy. Hobbes used Annabelle as his test subject. St. Luc realises that she may have infected many of the residents. Linsky agrees to meet St. Luc back at the complex. As the epidemic spreads, Betts is infected by a parasite that has crawled up through the plughole in her bath. The nurse, Forsythe, is attacked by another resident. She stabs the man, who flees just before St. Luc arrives. The doctor takes a sample of infected blood, and the pair head out into the corridor. St. Luc and Forsythe meet an elderly couple who have seen the parasite entering a chute to the basement. Forsythe stays with them while St. Luc goes to investigate. An infected man rushes him, but St. Luc escapes. Forsythe goes looking for the doctor, who she finds in Merrick's office, ordering the manager to call the police. Nick tries to have sex with Janine, but she feels the lumps in his stomach and runs out to Betts' apartment where her friend reveals amorous feelings for her. As they kiss, Betts passes the parasite to Janine. Arriving at the complex, Linsky finds Nick at home, his stomach writhing with multiple parasites, one of which assails Linsky. Nick kills the man and reclaims the parasite by pushing it into his mouth. In the basement, St. Luc saves Forsythe from being raped by a security guard, who he shoots. They hide, waiting for the police to arrive. When a parasite pushes out of Forsythe's mouth, St. Luc strikes her unconscious and carries her down a corridor. Through the walls, a wave of arms bursts out as hosts reach for the would-be escapees. St. Luc abandons Forsythe and runs to Tudor's apartment, where Nick has killed Linsky. St. Luc shoots Nick and tries to escape the building, but the exits are covered. The infection spreads, with gangs of residents marauding through the complex. St. Luc tries to escape via the indoor swimming pool and sees Betts and Janine making out in the water. He flees through the open patio door. Then hundreds of residents appear and force him back into the pool room, where he is pushed into the water and is overtaken by his infected neighbours. An orgy begins. Just before dawn, a convoy leaves Starliner Towers, St. Luc and Forsythe in one of the cars, heading for the city. A voice on the radio reveals a wave of violent sexual assaults in Montreal. The parasite is loose.

Comment

Shivers is Cronenberg's first professional film. Following two experimental features, he wanted to reach a bigger audience, yet he also desired to show the unshowable. And what a way to achieve that. In conservative 1970s Canada, which had just enjoyed a decade of sex comedies, *Shivers* came as a shock. This was especially true of its denouement, which some saw as bleak but Cronenberg regarded as hopeful, a happy ending. He identified with the parasite, which he has said was 'very vital, very excited, really having a good time'. The idea that a parasite was necessarily a bad thing is upended in *Shivers*. The film says that in adaptation, humanity gains a new perspective, a new idea of itself. Although their fate reminds us of Jack Finney's body snatchers, Cronenberg's characters seem to welcome the invader. Some of the performances are less than polished, adding to the impression of repressed characters numbed by consumerism. These people are ready for revelation.

They come alive when transformed and with the zeal of the converted, pass on their good fortune to everyone they meet. Although the parasite uses the host's secret desires to propagate itself, this is a symbiosis rather than a takeover, which will become a significant concept in the director's films. *Shivers* also gives us Hobbes, another early model for Cronenberg's outsider doctors and scientists.

Shivers turned out to be his calling card, starting a run of films that redefined the horror genre. Its idea of a scientifically engineered parasite designed to replace human organs, is one which *Rabid* would take much further.

Meanwhile, in Shepperton, J. G. Ballard had been writing a multi-storey novel, *High-Rise*, which examined some of the same themes as *Shivers*: an enclosed society turning in on itself, the breakdown of social norms, and the release of inner desires to destructive-creative effect. Neither artist was aware of the other's project; the fact that *Shivers* and *High-Rise* hold a mirror to each other reveals their creators' similar reading of the zeitgeist. The penultimate scene of *Shivers*, in which the protagonist's fate is decided, plays like a baptism, but reads like a particularly Ballardian kind of surrender.

Rabid (1977)

Production: Canadian Film Development Corporation, the Dibar Syndicate, Dunning/Link/Reitman, Famous Players Film Company, Sommerville House Releasing
Produced by John Dunning, André Link and Ivan Reitman
Cinematographer: René Verzier
Sound: Dan Goldberg and Richard Lightstone
Music Supervisor: Ivan Reitman
Special Effects: Joe Blasco Make-Up Association, Al Griswold, Byrd Holland
Written and directed by David Cronenberg
Filming dates: 1 November 1976 to 5 December 1976
US and Canadian release: 8 April 1977
UK release: 2 September 1977 (Edinburgh); 8 January 1978 (London)
Running time: 91 minutes
Budget: $180,000
Cast: Marilyn Chambers (Rose), Lynne Deragon (Nurse Louise), Patricia Gage (Dr Roxanne Keloid), Frank Moore (Hart Read), J. Roger Periard (Lloyd Walsh), Susan Roman (Mindy Kent), Howard Ryshpan (Dr Dan Keloid), Joe Silver (Murray Cypher)

Background

Rabid is the first 'straight' film of pornographic actress Marilyn Chambers, but that wasn't the original intention.

Having seen her in Terrence Malick's *Badlands*, Cronenberg had wanted Sissy Spacek for the part of Rose, but the producers weren't keen on her Texan accent or her freckles. Spacek went on to hit big in *Carrie* (1976), which came out while *Rabid* was still in production. In Cronenberg's film, Rose passes a cinema where *Carrie* is playing. An intentional nod or just a result of filming on location? Perhaps both.

Instead of Spacek, producer Ivan Reitman suggested Chambers, who wanted to break into legitimate film following her success in *Behind the Green Door*, and as the face of the Ivory Snow brand. Cronenberg screen-tested her and put her in the movie.

As mentioned, in *Rabid*, Chambers gets to penetrate the men. There's a scene in a porno cinema where she does just that, but Cronenberg said that he hadn't written the scene with an adult actress in mind. It was one of those ironies that happen in retrospect. Afterwards, he said he was impressed by her performance and thought that she could go on to pursue a mainstream career. This didn't work out, although she was up for several films, including projects by Nicholas Ray (whose film didn't get made) and George C. Scott (who thought she looked too wholesome to play a porno star in his movie).

Part-funded by a writing grant, *Rabid* confirmed Cronenberg's career choice as a filmmaker. If he had written the novel, he might never have made another film. For that reason alone, this is an important entry in his filmography.

Story

Hart Read and his girlfriend Rose are travelling in the countryside near Montreal
when they crash their motorbike into a camper van stopped in the middle of
the road. Hart is concussed, and his hand and shoulder are hurt. Rose is more
seriously injured, suffering burns. They are taken to the nearby Keloid Clinic for
Plastic Surgery. Doctor Dan Keloid decides that Rose needs immediate treatment.
He performs an experimental new surgery on her using morphogenetically
neutral grafts to repair her damaged organs, and Rose enters a coma. No one
is sure whether she will recover fully or if the grafts will give her cancer. Over a
month goes by. Hart has been released but Rose, still comatose, remains at the
clinic. When she wakes suddenly, screaming, a patient called Lloyd tries to calm
her, but as she holds on to him, she somehow pierces his right arm. He retains
no memory of the incident. The wound is unusual; the blood won't clot, and
Lloyd loses feeling in his right side. Dr Keloid has no idea of what caused this
injury and sends Lloyd to Montreal General for observation. Keloid's radical
procedure has caused Rose's body to mutate. From an orifice under her armpit,
a phallic proboscis emerges to puncture her victims for their blood. In search of
sustenance, she leaves the clinic and feeds on a cow on a nearby farm. This makes
her vomit; it is human blood that she needs. When a drunk farmer tries to assault
her, she punctures him and drinks his blood; he escapes. Rose calls Hart to come
and get her. Meanwhile, the farmer, now infected with Rose's 'rage', attacks a
waitress at a diner. The rage is breaking out elsewhere too. Lloyd leaves the
clinic and attacks the taxi driver taking him to the airport; the car crashes in the
freeway and is hit by a truck that kills both men. Back at the clinic, Rose infects
Keloid himself. Panic spreads throughout the facility as the epidemic grows.
Before Hart can collect her, Rose leaves the clinic and hitches rides from several
drivers on the way to the city. She infects one of the drivers, who attacks his co-
worker. Searching for Rose, Hart and Keloid's colleague, Murray Cypher, discuss
the burgeoning epidemic with police chief Claude LaPointe and some health
officials. A policeman is infected before being shot by a fellow officer. Hart calls
Mindy, a friend, and asks her to keep Rose indoors if she turns up. He will come
over to get her. Rose then arrives at Mindy's apartment to stay for a while. Mindy
watches a news item about a new strain of rabies terrorising Montreal. Rose goes
out to a sex cinema and infects a man in the audience. Chief LePointe and two
health officials are attacked in their limousine by infected building workers who
use a jackhammer to open the driver's door and feed on him. LePointe and one
of the health officials leave the driver behind, escaping in the limousine. The
infection now spreads quickly throughout the city; rabies treatments are not
working. Doctor Royce Gentry advises the authorities to introduce a shoot-to-kill
policy to slow the spread of the infection. He works on a cure as martial law is
declared, roadblocks are set up and soldiers, wearing protective suits, arrive on
the streets to dispose of the bodies. Hart leaves Cypher home. When Cypher calls
to his wife, no one replies, but in the nursery he finds the remains of his dead
baby. Then his wife appears and attacks him. Still searching for Rose, Hart goes

back to the city in Cypher's car and is attacked by an infected citizen. Soldiers shoot the attacker, disinfect the car with spray and send Hart on his way. Mindy, in her apartment, is still watching the news. A possible patient zero, who may be immune, has been traced to the Keloid Clinic. Rose comes in and punctures Mindy. Hart enters the apartment to find Rose feeding. He tries to convince her to get treatment, but she denies that she is the source. Hart chases her, but Rose knocks him unconscious and escapes. She pierces a man in the lobby of the building and drags him into his apartment, locking them both inside. Rose calls Hart, who has woken up. Her plan is to test Hart's hypothesis. If he is right, the man she has attacked should become infected and will kill her. Hart, distraught, tries to convince Rose to get away from the man. But Hart is powerless as he listens on the telephone. The man wakes up and kills Rose. The next morning, there's a strange sense of calm in the city as soldiers clearing corpses find Rose's body in the street. They dump it in their garbage truck and go on to round up more bodies. The implication is that this infection, this rage, has devastated the city. Rose's body is treated as just another piece of hazardous waste.

Comment

The story of *Rabid* is a spin on the vampire-zombie-epidemic genre that, like the best of these, has a social conscience. It takes the building-wide panic of *Shivers* and imagines it on the scale of a city, a natural progression given how the first film ends. One of his most recognisably Canadian films, with Québécois characters to the fore, *Rabid* has something to say. Through the mishandling of its fictional epidemic, the film satirises the government of the day. As well as this, a scene set in a police station where two First Nations people are given a breathalyser test, comments on society's failure to help indigenous people with issues such as alcoholism. The film's Canadian identity is, therefore, crucial to its aesthetic and its politics.

What most people will remember it for, perhaps, is Marilyn Chambers, who gives a good performance as Rose, but the bar isn't set particularly high here: the other actors are not great.

If it weren't for the different origin of the infection, *Rabid* could have been constructed as a direct sequel to *Shivers*, restating its themes before *The Brood*, his first brilliant film, gives them a personal emotional weight. *Rabid* doesn't feel as original as its predecessor but it does mark a progression of Cronenberg's psychosexual themes, and it's his first proper tragedy, all the better for the depressing ending. Rose's fate, undeserved, cruel and unavoidable, stands for the fate of a whole society. This time the parasite isn't transforming us for the better, at least from a human point of view.

Rabid scores particularly well with its ideas, which at the time might have seemed far-fetched and now appear far-seeing. Its plot is set in motion with what we would call stem cell therapy. *Rabid* also shows us a combination vulva-penis attack before *Alien* does. Not bad for a horror flick that exists just on the right side of exploitation.

Fast Company (1979)

Production: Canadian Film Development Corporation, Quadrant Films
Produced by Michael Lebowitz, Peter O'Brian, David M. Perlmutter, Courtney Smith
Screenplay by David Cronenberg, Phil Savath, Courtney Smith
Story by Alan Treen
Cinematographer: Mark Irwin
Music: Fred Mollin
Directed by David Cronenberg
Running time: 91 minutes
Filming dates: 21 July to 29 August 1978
Canada release: 18 March 1979
US release: 17 August 1979
Running time: 91 minutes
Cast: Nicholas Campbell (Billy Brooker), Judy Foster (Candy), Claudia Jennings (Sammy), John Saxon (Phil Adamson), Cedric Smith (Gary Black), William Smith (Lonnie Johnson)

Background

Fast Company was commissioned by producer Peter O'Brian, whose previous success was *Outrageous!*, a drag film of an entirely different sort. For Cronenberg, the project was an opportunity to show that he could work within the constraints of a mainstream genre while still making a personal picture. Although it is the first of his movies that he didn't originate, he had a hand in the script, sometimes getting up at five in the morning to do rewrites. Uniquely for a Cronenberg picture, the score includes soft rock songs, written and performed by Fred Mollin, whose successful career in music continues to this day.

Many of the cast are veteran character actors, which is a step up from the semi-amateur performances seen in earlier pictures. William Smith had a history of playing competitive losers in low-budget sports films, so he knew what he was doing. The late, great John Saxon was already a veteran of B-movies. *Playboy* playmate and adult movie star Claudia Jennings shines in this, her final role before her death in a car crash.

Filmed at the old speedway in Edmonton, as well as other places in Alberta, *Fast Company* is Cronenberg's first work with cinematographer Mark Irwin, and the improvement in visual quality shows. It is also his introduction to other collaborators who would stay with him for many years, including production designer Carol Spier and editor Ronald Sanders.

Story

Celebrated drag racing star Lonnie Johnson is checking his 'funny car' at a racetrack. He's here to test drive the vehicle, which is sponsored by Fast Company, a multinational oil corporation. Johnson is their star driver. During the run, the car burns up, but Johnson, nicknamed 'Lucky Man' for a reason,

41

emerges without a scratch. As this goes on, Fast Co. team leader Phil Adamson tells Elder, the head mechanic, that if repairs are too expensive, the company can't afford to crash while winning races. He wants the car in good shape to keep the Fast Co. brand out there selling cans of oil. Next, in a thrilling race, Johnson's protégé Billy Brooker takes on rival star driver Gary Black, and although Billy loses, he shows promise. The team moves on to a meet at Big Sky, Montana. Lonnie calls his girl, Sammy, who lives in Spokane, and they agree to meet soon. When the Fast Co. rig pops a tyre, Black and his team come along and grudgingly agree to help, but after an argument with Lonnie, Gary Black withdraws that offer. Meanwhile, Adamson flies his private plane to the race meeting, accompanied by Candy Ellison, the new advertising girl for Fast Company. He puts his hand on her knee, but she brushes him off. Arriving at the track, Adamson takes a backhander from the race organiser as payment for replacing Billy Brooker in the upcoming race with Johnson. The fans have come to see the star driver, and Johnson's own car is in the shop. Neither driver is happy with this turn of events, and Brooker blames Johnson's ego for the switch. Johnson races Black, who is also against this change of driver especially if it means he loses to his rival. After the race, Billy finds himself a little happier when he hooks up with Candy. Johnson's next race is in Spokane, where Sammy is due to join him. On the way, he calls the mechanic with suggestions on how to fix his dragster but learns that Adamson has cancelled the repair. At Spokane, a furious Lonnie does a TV interview in which he sarcastically disrespects Fast Co. and its products. Incensed, Adamson phones his bosses to say that he is bringing Gary Black in to replace Johnson. Candy, having just entered his office, overhears him. Then, because she refuses to have sex with the TV interviewer to smooth things over after Johnson's unruly interview, Adamson fires her. He offers Black the Fast Co. spot in the race, which Black accepts. Inside Johnson's trailer, Candy and Billy go to bed. When Sammy arrives, she's shocked, assuming it's Lonnie in bed with Candy, until Lonnie also arrives. Billy and Candy leave, then the reunited lovers hit the sack. Not long after, Adamson walks in unannounced, interrupting them, to fire Lonnie. During the ensuing argument, Lonnie insists he will race again. He punches Adamson and makes him leave. Outside, Adamson approaches Gary Black and his mechanic, named Meatball, asking them to do something for him. Testing the car once more, Johnson saves himself when the engine blows and he escapes uninjured. Billy accuses Black of sabotage, but Lonnie takes Black's side. Why would an established driver such as Gary Black need to do such a thing? Back at the pit, Adamson follows through on his plan, firing Lonnie's team and introducing Black as his new star driver. As Lonnie goes to attack Adamson, Meatball knocks him unconscious. All seems lost. Billy is upset, but Lonnie has an idea of how they can still go to the next meet in Edmonton with their funny car. First, they need to find it. When Billy and his friend P. J. attend a motor show, they are surprised to see the car there, Adamson showing it off. The same night,

Billy and Candy drive in front of the building where the car is being kept and distract the security guard by kissing each other and exposing one of Candy's breasts. Meanwhile, Lonnie breaks in and drives the funny car away. Candy and Billy make a fast exit, leaving the security guard nonplussed. Lonnie, Billy and P. J. work through the night to get the car ready for the race. Arriving at the track in Edmonton, Lonnie enters his team as independents. Adamson is there, worried that his former star will beat Black. Meatball reassures him that Black will win if he stays in the left lane. It seems that Lonnie is going to take the car, but he steps back and, conscious of his role as a mentor, gives it to Billy, who is both surprised and overjoyed. Billy wins the coin-toss to pick lanes and chooses the left one. However, Adamson has the lane changed, and Billy has no choice but to take the right lane. The drivers put their cars into position, ready to go. Gary Black watches as Meatball walks off the track, carrying two oil cans. The cars zoom away and Black takes the lead, driving dirty to swerve in front of Billy. Before he can change course, Black's car skids on the oil that Meatball has poured across the left lane. His car blows up. Billy stops his car and goes after Meatball. As they fight, Meatball's clothes catch fire, and Billy grabs his extinguisher to put the flames out. Meatball's life is saved, but Gary Black is dead. As the team reaches the scene of the crash, Adamson runs to his plane and tries to take off. Lonnie jumps in his funny car and gives chase. When he catches up with Adamson's plane, he clips the wing. The aircraft takes off, but Adamson loses control and crashes into a Fast Co. tanker, which explodes, killing him. The next day, the newly forged team has gathered. Lonnie promises to get funding for them. He and Sammy are first going to share some time together. Billy and Candy decide to do the same. The couples go off separately to find somewhere to make love as Elder and P. J., ever the professionals, turn to the business of preparing the car.

Comment

Building on themes in his TV short, *The Italian Machine* (1976), which features a motorcycle heist, *Fast Company* is honest in its pleasures. It is also probably of most interest to the director himself, a car enthusiast and sometime racer.

Although a detour from his usual horror, *Fast Company* is an interesting film in the Cronenberg canon, simply because it is so different from the others. There are no creepy penis-monsters here, unless you count the men. There's no body horror, unless you consider the merging of driver and machine as a means to a fiery end. Sometimes these drivers come across as cyborgs, so tightly are they bound to their vehicles. *Fast Company* does exactly what it says on the tin: it's a melodrama about racing. The tropes are present and correct. A veteran racer faces his inevitable replacement by a rising young star. The old guy wins one last shot at the big time to show that he's still got it. Then, on his own terms, he hands the reins to the pretender. Along the way, he socks it to the Man, gets laid, has fistfights, fixes something mechanical, proves himself to himself, and gets laid again. Change the sport and *Fast Company* could easily be a boxing movie or a wrestling picture, with much the same story. Stallone built his career on such material.

Beautifully shot, the film is blessed with Irwin's camera and Cronenberg's direction as they fetishise the cars, the men, the women, the need for speed. There are fisticuffs. There is an underhanded villain. There is female nudity. There is male violence. Not only does the director take this film seriously, he enjoys it, which is also what the audience is meant to do. *Fast Company* has a very 'Me' generation way with free love as a reward for a man's hard work, and you can smell the Blue Stratos mixed in with the heady fuelled-up atmosphere, making for a cocktail that couldn't be more macho if it also contained Bourbon and testosterone.

Depending on your expectations, *Fast Company* is a fun movie, but if you're looking for polymorphous autoeroticism along with your car fetish, you might want to wait seventeen years for the next one.

The Brood (1979)

Production: Canadian Film Development Corporation, Elgin International Films and Mutual Productions
Produced by Pierre David, Claude Heroux and Victor Solnicki
Cinematographer: Mark Irwin
Music: Howard Shore
Written and directed by David Cronenberg
Filming dates: 14 November 1978 to 21 December 1978
Canada release: 1 June 1979
US release: 25 May 1979
UK release: 13 March 1980
Running time: 92 minutes
Budget: CAD$1.5 million
Cast: Samantha Eggar (Nola Carveth), Art Hindle (Frank Carveth), Cindy Hinds (Candice Carveth), Susan Hogan (Ruth Mayer), Oliver Reed (Dr Hal Raglan)

Background

Nobody expected *Fast Company*. Nor did many expect David Cronenberg to keep making that kind of film. He might have followed an increasingly commercial path but in the breakdown of his marriage and the custody battle that followed, *The Brood* was born. Having heard about *Kramer vs Kramer*, Cronenberg was disillusioned by its apparent optimism. In *The Brood*, he released his own psychic children in an undeniably heartfelt nightmare.

All of Cronenberg's films are personal, but *The Brood* was the first to reveal the shape of his rage, as it were. In many ways, it's his most extreme work. The structure is that of a classical horror story, down to the hero entering the lair to confront the monster, and the sacrifices required to earn a resolution. Fuelled by anger and pain, Cronenberg gave Nola some of the characteristics he had seen in his ex-wife. He wrote what he hoped would be an honest description of his experience, viewed through the lens of horror.

In *The Brood*, he assembles his first cast of name actors. Oliver Reed had form with outré pictures, having worked with Ken Russell (*Women in Love*, *The Devils*). Samantha Eggar, veteran Shakespearean and film actress, was not shy of unsettling material either, memorably playing Miranda opposite Terence Stamp in William Wyler's *The Collector*. Impressed by the screenplay, Eggar found that she could not turn down the role of Nola. Eggar and Reed had grown up beside each other in England and had worked together before. These connections enrich their chemistry in the film.

Art Hindle, fresh off *Invasion of the Body Snatchers*, played Nola's husband, Frank. Eight-year-old Cindy Hinds, in her first film role, portrayed their daughter Candice. The children of Nola's rage were played by girls from a local school gymnastics group.

Starting on 14 November 1978, *The Brood* filmed until December in Toronto, with additional filming in Mississauga, Ontario. It was a lean shoot with a small crew. Eggar says that her scenes were done in three days.

One name that must be mentioned is Howard Shore. His score is suitably dark and full of menace. This is a watershed moment, Shore's music going on to become, with one exception, an essential element that gives Cronenberg's films their character.

Although *The Brood* is about a family, it is not a family film but a mad masterpiece of horror and gore, so it's not surprising that censors asked for cuts in the US, Canada and the UK. One excision hurt. Eggar, relishing her performance, decided to lick the rage-foetuses as they emerged, like a cat licking her kittens as soon as they're born. Cronenberg agreed and shot a 'long and loving close-up of Samantha licking the foetus'. This scene was cut, with the result that 'a lot of people thought she was eating her baby'. The movie came out uncensored on home video decades later, and viewers can now judge the scene for themselves.

Premiering on 1 June 1979 in Toronto and Chicago, *The Brood* went on to do well at the box office, covering its costs several times over.

Critics were in two minds. Variety called it 'extremely well made' but 'essentially unpleasant'. Leonard Maltin was appalled. 'Eggar eats her own afterbirth while midget clones beat grandparents and lovely young schoolteachers to death with mallets. It's a big, wide, wonderful world we live in!' Some commentators considered it 'sickening' and 'irresponsible'. Robin Wood branded it 'reactionary', in that it 'portrays feminine power as irrational and horrifying'. Whatever the critics thought at the time, *The Brood* outlasted all opprobrium to become regarded as Cronenberg's first mature classic.

Story

At the Somafree institute, Dr Hal Raglan has developed a new psychotherapeutic technique called psychoplasmics. This approach entices mentally ill patients to release their inner turmoil by expressing emotions physically. Feelings are translated into physiological effects, showing up as changes in the patient's body.

Nola Carveth is a patient of Dr Raglan. She is intensely disturbed, her condition not helped by a custody battle with her husband, Frank. Their five-year-old daughter Candice is caught between the warring parents.

Following a visit with her mother, Candice shows bruises on her body and Frank decides to stop Nola's visitation rights. Dr Raglan responds by intensifying her treatment, to return her to mental wellbeing as soon as possible. In their therapy sessions, the doctor learns that Nola was physically and emotionally abused by her mother, who was violent and an alcoholic. Her father, in denial, failed to intervene to protect the girl.

Frank wants to disprove the utility of Raglan's experiments, and he seeks out a former patient of the Somafree Institute, Jan Hartog, who is dying of lymphoma brought on by having been treated with psychoplasmics.

Juliana, Nola's mother, takes Candice for the evening while Frank is away. As they spend the time looking at old photos, Juliana tells her granddaughter that when Nola was a girl, she was often hospitalised due to strange marks on her skin. Doctors were mystified.

In the kitchen, a dwarf-like child-creature attacks Juliana, killing her with a round of vicious blows. Candice is disturbed but the creature leaves her physically unharmed.

Barton, Juliana's former husband, comes for the funeral and tries to see Nola at the Institute, but Raglan won't allow it.

Some days later Frank invites Ruth Mayer, Candice's teacher, to dinner to discuss her concerns about how the girl is doing in school. Barton phones up, drunk, insisting that Frank and he go to Somafree to confront Raglan and see Nola. Frank takes pity on the bereaved man, and leaves Candice with Ruth.

After Frank has gone, the telephone rings. Ruth answers and hears Nola on the other end. Nola immediately assumes that Ruth and Frank are having an affair. She warns the teacher angrily to stay away from her family.

At Barton's house, Frank finds the man murdered by the dwarf-child-creature, who then attempts to kill him but dies before it can succeed. Frank calls the police.

The autopsy shows that the creature has several physiological differences from human anatomy. It has no navel, for one thing, so it can't have been born naturally.

When the story makes the news, Raglan admits that Nola's psychoplasmics sessions may have influenced the nature of the murders carried out by the creature. He agrees to close the Somafree Institute and sends most of his patients into the care of the city, but keeps Nola for himself. She's unfinished business.

Hartog tells Frank that Somafree has been shuttered. One of the other patients who have had to leave the institute, says that Nola is Raglan's 'queen bee'. She's in charge of the dwarf-children who live in Somafree's attic.

In school, two of those children arrive and kill Ruth as she teaches, then they kidnap Candice and take her to the institute. Frank sets off in pursuit.

At Somafree, Frank confronts Raglan, and the doctor reveals the truth about the children. They are an unintended consequence of Nola's psychoplasmics therapy, born out of her intense rage. Psychoplasmics expresses feelings in physical form; the creatures are Nola's emotions made flesh. They attack the sources of her distress, assaulting those for whom she feels anger. Nola has never been aware of this; she is innocent of the murders carried out by her 'children'.

Dr Raglan realises that the children are a threat to anyone who upsets Nola, so he decides to go into their attic and rescue Candice. Frank must keep Nola calm to give Raglan a chance to succeed without being attacked.

Frank pretends to try making up with Nola, resolving their differences and repairing their marriage. As they talk, Nola shows him her external womb, from

47

which another child is being born. Frank's expression of disgust alerts her to his duplicity and in her anger, Nola threatens to kill Candice rather than have her taken away. Provoked by her rage, the brood-creatures in the attic kill Dr Raglan then turn on Candice. The girl finds a hiding place in a cupboard and closes the door, but it doesn't take long before her 'siblings' start to break through.

Fearing for his daughter, Frank strangles Nola and the brood dies with her. He goes to the attic to get Candice – who is now seriously disturbed – and brings her to his car. As Frank drives her to safety, two rage-lesions are visible on Candice's arm.

Comment

If you know the context for the character, it is clear that Nola Carveth, the mother of the brood, is written in the shape of the director's own rage, expressing anger at his ex-wife in the aftermath of their custody battle. It's not pretty, but it was cathartic for him. So, how does this explosion of familial horror work on the screen? Creepily, is one word. Unforgettable is another. This is where his film career matures with a drama about a couple separating. It just happens to have rage-babies going around killing innocent people. These creatures evoke *Don't Look Now* (1973), which seems intentional, as Roeg's masterpiece is one of the films that Cronenberg considers terrifying.

The Brood is both a deep psychological mind-trip and a gruesome monster flick, with the monster being the product of psychotherapy. Like some sort of quantum entanglement, *The Brood* activates *A Dangerous Method* thirty years in the future. It calls out to *Dead Ringers* a decade on. It even helps to seed *The Fly*, for what is Brundlefly except a child of hubris and anger? Some of Cronenberg's best pictures are about the separation of couples: siblings, husband and wife, a diplomat and his butterfly, a human and a proto-fly... a thread first spun in *The Brood*.

Another idea that matures in *The Brood* is that the characters are both perpetrators and victims, complicit in their own derangement. Nola is a monster, but she doesn't know it. Hal Raglan, her Frankenstein, knows it but keeps going despite reports of red-coated homunculi killing the people in Nola's life. Raglan is a good example of the Cronenberg doctor. To such a character, the method, the experiment, is more important to humanity than the life of one person. He has good intentions but what he doesn't reckon with are the lengths to which Nola's anger-children will go to protect her.

Having spoken about how satisfying it was to have Frank strangle Nola at the end, does the director allow the audience any compassion for her? Despite everything, and like Rose before her, she deserves at least some. Nola is suffering in a way her husband could never imagine.

The director's sympathy seems to lie with Frank, a decent everyman mystified by the strange events that have overtaken his family. When his daughter is abducted to live with her monster-spawning mother, under the control of a cult-like community where a mastermind-guru exposes her to a dangerous form of psychotherapy, it's not so far from what happened in real life. Just as art can help calm the psyche of its creator, *The Brood* is Cronenberg's safety valve.

And what of the child caught up in the storm? The final scene reveals the film's true meaning and its director's greatest fear when he was making it, that this story will never be over.

Scanners (1981)

Production: Canadian Film Development Corporation, Filmplan International Inc.
Produced by Pierre David, Claude Heroux and Victor Solnicki
Cinematographer: Mark Irwin
Music: Howard Shore
Written and directed by David Cronenberg
Filming dates: 30 October to 23 December 1979
Canada release: 16 January 1981
US release: 14 January 1981
UK release: 23 April 1981
Running time: 103 minutes
Budget: $3.5 million
Cast: Lawrence Dane (Braedon Keller), Michael Ironside (Darryl Revok), Stephen Lack (Cameron Vale), Patrick McGoohan (Dr Paul Ruth), Jennifer O'Neill (Kim Obrist)

Background

Scanners has its roots in a treatment that David Cronenberg developed in 1976, called *Telepathy 2000*, a logical next step after *Rabid*. However, *Fast Company* and *The Brood* came first, and the project waited four years. That early treatment featured a lead called Harley Quinn, who telepathically rapes a woman. The character's name indicates that Cronenberg was inspired by the world of comic books, with the X-Men being a possible influence on this story. Senders, hostile telepaths from Burroughs's *Naked Lunch*, were another. *Telepathy 2000* would have been a spy film, featuring competing good and evil psychic agents.

When *Scanners* began shooting in 1980, neither the sets nor the script were finished. The film had been rushed into production with less than two months allowed, the producers having seen an opportunity to qualify for a tax write-off. Consequently, Cronenberg was forced to write scenes in the mornings before filming. According to the director, this was one of his most difficult films to make.

Locations were found in Montreal and Toronto. As in *Stereo* and *Crimes of the Future*, *Scanners* uses modern public buildings to give it a sense of taking place 'five minutes into the future'. The Tour Future Electronique, a high-rise by the Saint Charles river in Québec, stood in for the ConSec HQ, and a water-treatment plant represented the base of Bicarbon Amalgamate. For the 'exploding head' scene at the ConSec presentation, a lecture hall in Concordia University was used.

Making heads into weapons was not new to make-up artist Dick Smith, who had worked on *The Exorcist*. In that film, Regan's possessed body ignored the rules of both physics and pilates. For *Scanners*, Smith built the exploding head, helping to create one of the most famous migraines in cinema history. He and his team made a plaster skull with a gelatin exterior crafted to look like the victim's head. They stuffed it with projectile detritus: latex, wax, bits of hamburger. Mounting this on the body of a dummy, they intended to set off an explosion remotely. None of these attempts worked but Gary Zeller, the special effects supervisor, had an idea. He asked the crew to roll camera then secure themselves inside the production trucks. He then hid behind the desk and fired a shotgun up at the prosthetic head. It worked.

It's this scene that gives the film its reputation. On its release in 1981, Roger Ebert praised the effects but compared *Scanners* unfavourably with Ken Russell's contemporaneous *Altered States*. '... on the level of its technical credits, *Scanners* is a fully qualified thriller. What matters is that *Altered States* involved its characters in experiences that we believed (for the length of the movie) were really happening to them.'

Story

In a city where psychics are real, they have become a resource to be exploited. ConSec, a company that develops weapons, has gathered interested parties in an auditorium to show off its new mind-killer. Scanners are capable of a range of telepathic and psychokinetic powers, affecting human minds and machines alike. The company's representative asks for a volunteer on which the ConSec scanner will demonstrate his power, stopping short of damage. The volunteer, a man called Darryl Revok, unexpectedly fights back. With the power of his mind, he makes the ConSec scanner's head explode as if a shotgun had blown it away. Pandemonium breaks out, and making his escape, Revok kills the officials who try to arrest him.

Revok has a scar on his forehead, the result of auto-surgery to release his psychic powers. His attack is a major setback for ConSec, and it seems to be a declaration of war.

At a meeting to discuss the crisis, ConSec's security chief, Keller, says the company should end the scanner program. But Dr Paul Ruth, head of research, argues that the incident with Revok surely illustrates the potential for this new weapon. Ruth seems to know Revok, the prime mover behind the assassination, who runs his own underground scanner network. Instead of shutting down the scanners, Ruth proposes infiltrating Revok's group to destabilise it from within.

He happens to have the perfect agent: Cameron Vale, a scanner whose untrained power has turned him into a homeless outcast and driven him mad. The doctor injects Vale with a drug, Ephemerol, which returns him to a calm state of mind while stopping his ability to scan. This change is not permanent and the drug must be taken periodically to give Vale control over his gift. What Ruth needs, in return, is Vale's help. Revok is killing any scanner who won't join him, but Ruth can teach Vale to use his power to save them all.

However, there's a mole in ConSec: its security head, Keller. He tells Revok about Ruth's plan to infiltrate the underground scanner network using Vale. Revok sends assassins after Vale, who is visiting the scanner artist Benjamin

Pierce in search of information on Revok's whereabouts. The assassins attack, shooting Pierce. Angered, Vale kills some of them with his telepathic power and as Pierce dies from his injuries, Vale picks up a name from inside the man's mind: Kim Obrist.

Vale goes to find Obrist, who is part of a telepathically aligned band of scanners who oppose Revok and his renegades. When Revok's assassins attack Obrist's group, all but she and Vale are killed. From scanning one of the assassins Vale learns about a pharmaceutical company that might be behind all of this.

Infiltrating this organisation, he finds that stocks of Ephemerol are being sent around the country through a computer program that Revok runs via ConSec. Returning to ConSec, Obrist and Vale meet Ruth, who tells Vale to scan the computer system to find out what he needs to know. Then Keller enters, attacking Obrist and killing Ruth.

As Vale and Obrist make their escape, he scans the computer 'cyberpathically' via a telephone line. He extracts information about Ephemerol shipments. Keller, newly motivated, orders the computer turned off while Vale is on the other end of the scan, to damage Vale when the signal is cut. Instead, the computer explodes, killing the security chief.

Now Vale and his new comrade follow up on the Ephemerol recipients. While visiting a doctor on the list, Obrist realises that a foetus somewhere in the room has scanned her. If a foetus can scan, Ephemerol must cause that ability when given to pregnant women. Revok and his henchmen arrive to abduct Vale and Obrist.

Back at Revok's base, Obrist is kept in another room as Revok reveals the whole story to Vale. Dr Ruth developed Ephemerol as a tranquilliser to treat pregnant women. The side effects became clear to him when he gave the most powerful dose of the drug to his own wife. Revok and Vale are, in fact, brothers, and Ruth is their father. The two sons, thanks to the high quantities of Ephemerol their mother received, are the most powerful scanners in the world. Revok intends to mass-produce Ephemerol so that doctors, unaware of the effects, will prescribe it to their pregnant patients. These psychically gifted offspring, with Revok as their leader, will take over the world. When Vale refuses Revok's offer to join them, they battle fiercely using their minds. Revok burns Vale's body to a cinder-husk collapsed on the ground.

Obrist comes in and sees Vale's ashen corpse. Then she hears his voice. It's coming from Revok, who cowers in a corner, his back to her. Revok turns, and she sees that he has lost the scar on his forehead. To save himself, Vale took over Revok's mind as his own body burned. Vale-as-Revok turns to Kim Obrist and says, 'We've won'.

Comment

The idea of telepathic mind control is not new, but what *Scanners* does is give it a personality. Burroughs said that language is a virus; Cronenberg tells us that thoughts are too. Ideas can go viral, sent out as the malevolent impulses of these terrible, lost humans with their weaponised brains. Revok as a descendent of the characters in *Stereo* and *Crimes of the Future*? *Scanners* takes ideas from those pictures but more importantly, it previews the signal in *Videodrome*, becoming a conduit between Cronenberg's first experiments and the flowering of their effects.

One of the most notorious hooks in SF cinema, the exploding head, welcomes us to the world of *Scanners*, but it is still just an attention grabber. What's interesting is the story of outcasts who possess special powers, with which they try to reshape society. *Scanners* has been called an allegory for what happens when the counterculture goes mainstream. That idea works better in *Videodrome* and *Crash.*

Not Cronenberg's finest film, *Scanners* is nonetheless one of his most memorable, and a notable entry in the history of science fiction cinema. It helped usher in a style of pulp-trash SF that ran through the 1980s and beyond, from *The Terminator*, to *They Live*, to *Screamers*, to *Strange Days*. The film also has sociological resonance, with scanner factions recognisable as terrorists, vigilantes, survivalists, religious cults, or certain political parties. A modern film that takes this idea to extremes is John Hyams' extraordinary, and extraordinarily brutal, *Universal Soldier: Day of Reckoning*. In this art-slaughterhouse film, a cult of genetically modified super-soldiers, discarded by society, plan to take the fight to the norms. That seems very Revok, who is himself very Magneto.

There's a degree of nominative determinism in the surname of lead actor Stephen Lack as Cameron Vale, though it's possible that he was directed to give a blank performance reflective of Vale's predicament. The true star of *Scanners* is Michael Ironside, with his outsize showing as the monstrous Revok, his name one letter away from that of a tape machine, Revox. As an actor, Patrick McGoohan was a fine choice to play the shady Dr Paul Ruth, but not so much behind the scenes: he disagreed creatively with his director and there was much tension on set.

The gross-out moments are great, Dick Smith's prosthetics especially so, but no one here is as interesting as Nola Carveth or Hal Raglan. *Scanners* is more about its ideas than its characters.

For all its faults, *Scanners* is a key work in Cronenberg's filmography, marking the end of a phase. Between this and his next film, there is an enormous leap in the quality of his material and its execution. *Scanners* is where he prepares to take it.

Videodrome (1983)

Production: Canadian Film Development Corporation, Famous Players Limited, Filmplan International
Produced by: Pierre David, Claude Héroux, Lawrence Nesis, Victor Solnicki
Cinematographer: Mark Irwin
Music: Howard Shore
Special Effects: Rick Baker and Frank Carere
Written and directed by David Cronenberg
Filming dates: October to December 1981
Canada release: 4 February 1983
US release: 4 February 1983
UK release: 25 November 1983
Running time: 103 minutes
Budget: $5.9 million
Cast: Les Carlson (Barry Convex), Jack Creley (Brian O'Blivion), Peter Dvorsky (Harlan), Lynne Gorman (Masha), Deborah Harry (Nicki Brand), Sonja Smits (Bianca O'Blivion), James Woods (Max Renn)

Background

As a boy, David Cronenberg was curious about the television signals his set would pick up from across the border in the US Would they show him something he shouldn't see? Is there ever anything that shouldn't be seen? At his university, one of the lecturers was Marshall McLuhan, who inspired the character of Brian O'Blivion, media guru and prognosticator. Having turned down *Return of the Jedi*, Cronenberg decided to make an original story. *Videodrome* was one of his pitches to Pierre David, who had produced *Scanners*. For this next film, Cronenberg cast James Woods, a fan of his work, as Max Renn; and Deborah Harry as Nicki Brand. Harry was the singer with Blondie and was relatively new to movies. They both proved to be perfect for their roles. In Harry, Cronenberg followed his tradition of casting relative newcomers alongside more experienced actors. The effects in the film were devised by Rick Baker, who had worked on *An American Werewolf in London*. Howard Shore composed a dark orchestral score descending into electronic madness, reflecting the decline of Max Renn's relationship with reality. Shooting began in October 1981 and lasted until December, in Toronto. The Cathode Ray Mission is set in the Factory Theatre on Bathurst, a theatre dedicated to producing only Canadian material. Cronenberg filmed two alternative endings, one of which had Max and Nicki meeting on the *Videodrome* TV show set, which he called his 'happy ending'. He cut it because it implied a kind of afterlife, at odds with his own atheism. After its release, *Videodrome* was well-received. It was a *New York Times* Critic's Pick, with Janet Maslin praising James Woods' performance: '…his offhand wisecracking gives the performance a sharply authentic edge'.

Story

Max Renn is always looking for extreme content to show on CIVIC-TV, his underground Toronto station, which specialises in the obscene. Jaded with the softcore porn and hard violence he feeds the viewers, Max needs something with an edge. The illegal satellite dish that feeds CIVIC-TV by pulling in broadcasts from around the world is operated by a man named Harlan, who calls Max in to show him something new. What Harlan has discovered is insane. It's a television show called *Videodrome*, unscripted, depicting the torture and murder of real people. The signal appears to be coming from Malaysia. Max is amazed at how real the show looks. It's a brilliant simulation and Max believes it to be the future of television. He tells Harlan to start putting it out on CIVIC-TV.

Having been exposed to *Videodrome*, Max now begins to experience hallucinations, the lines between reality and television becoming blurred.

When he appears on a talk show to defend CIVIC-TV, Max meets Nicki Brand, a radio psychiatrist. She is intrigued by Max, though also somewhat repelled. The other guest on the show is Professor Brian O'Blivion, a prophet of the McLuhan variety, pushing 'the medium is the message' to its logical conclusion. He has agreed to take part in this discussion only via his image broadcast from elsewhere to a TV screen set up in the studio. For O'Blivion, this is him in person: he only ever appears 'on television'. He predicts that one day, television will become more real than real life.

Nicki and Max begin dating. He shows her *Videodrome*, a scene in which a woman is being tortured. Nicki becomes aroused, proving more open to experience than Max thinks he is, by goading him into having S&M sex while they watch the show.

At a meeting with Harlan, Max learns that *Videodrome* is not being broadcast from Malaysia after all, but Pittsburgh. The Malaysian signal is a cover to divert the authorities from the real source.

In his apartment, Max tells Nicki where *Videodrome* is based, and she's excited. She wants to appear on the show. Max is afraid for her but Nicki, to demonstrate how serious she is, puts a cigarette out on her breast. She's determined to audition for *Videodrome*. Pretending it's a business trip, Nicki goes to Pittsburgh. Max never sees her again in the real world.

Now he needs to find out what's going on. Who is behind *Videodrome*? He meets Masha, a fellow pornographer, to see if she can help him find the truth about the show. Masha informs him that the footage is real, not faked. Those people are being tortured and killed in the most excruciating ways. *Videodrome* is not just a television show, it's a front for a political movement, and Brian O'Blivion is involved.

Max finds O'Blivion's base at a vagrant shelter called the Cathode Ray Mission, a cult-like place where homeless people are made to watch television in long stretches, as therapy. The mission is run by Bianca O'Blivion, daughter of Brian. She intends to realise her father's goal of replacing all aspects of everyday life with television. Brian now exists only on thousands of videocassettes, recorded in the year before his death, from which his living essence can be simulated on TV.

Max sees a videotape in which O'Blivion reveals that *Videodrome* is a theatre of war, with factions fighting to control the minds of the population. Now, everything changes. Max begins to hallucinate, including a transformation in which a vaginal VCR slot appears in his torso.

Bianca explains to Max that he's experiencing side effects of having received the *Videodrome* signal, which induces a tumour in the viewer. Her father helped invent this technology, intending to advance his vision for society, but his partners wanted to use it for evil. When he tried to stop them, they killed him with his own invention.

The producers of *Videodrome* now reveal themselves. Spectacular Optical, a glasses company, fronts a weapons maker. Barry Convex, the head of this organisation, has been working alongside Harlan to infect Max with the *Videodrome* signal and get him to put it out on CIVIC-TV. Their intention is to use fatal tumours to kill those they see as undesirables: television watchers hooked on porn and violence. Convex inserts a videotape into Max's stomach slit. The tape is designed to brainwash him to do Convex's bidding.

Back at CIVIC-TV, Max kills his colleagues. He goes to the Cathode Ray Mission to kill Bianca, but she stops him by showing him a tape of Nicki being killed. Bianca then counter-brainwashes Max to make him attack *Videodrome*. Under her influence, he uses a 'flesh gun' to kill both Harlan and Barry Convex at a trade show for Spectacular Optical. He flees the scene and makes his way to the docks, where he finds an abandoned boat and goes inside to hide. Down in the cabin, he sees a television set on which Nicki now appears, saying that she's working to defeat *Videodrome*. To complete her victory, she must 'leave the old flesh'. Max watches as the television cuts to an image of him on this very boat, holding a gun to his head, crying out 'Long live the new flesh!', and shooting himself.

Repeating exactly what he has just seen on television, Max holds a gun to his head, cries out 'Long live the new flesh!' and shoots himself.

Comment

Videodrome is a perfect Cronenberg movie. It's also one of the most subversive science fiction films of the last forty years. Displaying a new sophistication, the writer-director blended body horror with a detached, intellectual aesthetic that went on to inform his mature style. *Videodrome*'s audacity and creative confidence took its director's reputation to new heights, as evinced by the contemporary retrospective at the Toronto International Film Festival, and the publication of *The Shape of Rage*. No longer seen as simply a horrormeister, Cronenberg was now taken seriously as an artist.

That word is not too strong. *Videodrome* is a compelling work, one that happens to be funny, sexy, violent, political, wild, and sometimes incoherent if you don't know where to look. It outdoes *The Thing* (1982) in its gleeful application of gore and outrageous design. It has imagination to burn, and it sears an indelible impression on the viewer's memory. The new flesh is alive, and reality television has never been so surreal.

When David Cronenberg originates a story rather than adapts one, the result seems somehow purer. In *Videodrome*, the dream logic of the story rips up the boundary between what is experienced and what's imagined. It encourages the viewer to go with the psychotropic flow, unclear when the suspension of disbelief becomes moot, and the hallucinations start. Is it when Renn first catches the *Videodrome* signal? Or when he sees the Betamax-vagina in his stomach? (Is Max himself named after the format?) The film asks how real Renn is anyway, compared with the 'unreality star' Brian O'Blivion, whose condition for existence is that he does so only on television. O'Blivion has the best fake-Irish name ever, which hints that Cronenberg is having fun making this stuff up.

James Woods injects just the right amount of sleaze into his performance. In later films, he would play a variation on the character. Lenny in *The Boost* (1988) is almost Renn-as-yuppie.

Videodrome is all about the screen. If the future that the film imagines is analogue, it is no more quaint than, say, the one predicted in *Alien*, also pre-digital, also timeless. In *Videodrome*, CRT tubes and videotapes bring the media apocalypse. Today we have people attacking 5G masts for fear that the technology might transmit Covid-19 through the medium of the air. In *Videodrome,* the signal is sent via cable TV. A relaxed viewer can overlook the obsolescence and enjoy the transistor-punk adventure. What matters, ironically, is not the medium, but the message. O'Blivion's statement that 'after all there is nothing real outside our perception of reality' seems today like a truism. How can we say for sure that he is wrong? 'The television screen has become the retina of the mind's eye', another of his sayings, describes perfectly a fact of life in modern society. The screen is inside us. We are cameras. We don't change the channels; the channels change us.

Videodrome's shock tactics might have been disturbing for some, exciting for others, but the film has a serious point. A comment on those who would attack free speech, the film has its cake and eats it by exposing the limits of both free expression and the desire to expunge it. Renn's persecutors use him as a guinea pig for a signal that will cause tumours, which is their response to content they dislike. The fundamentalists in *Videodrome* consider Renn a sick pornographer, so they feel justified in using the most extreme torture porn to attract his eyeballs before slicing them. It's very Republican, very Gilead. It's very now. This kind of entrapment has gone on for centuries, and although the Inquisition's torturers are not known to have used television, they would find *Videodrome*'s New Flesh a familiar kind of mortification.

As a satire on censorship, *Videodrome* is relevant today, with its themes of cancel culture, prurience, and the relationship between politics and the media.

If religion is the opium of the masses, *Videodrome* is the cocaine, and we're taking it all the time.

One of the many revelations in this film is the performance of Deborah Harry as Nicki Brand, who does indeed live up to the name, branding her breast with a lit cigarette. Harry is wonderful in a role that you'd imagine many full-time actors of the day would have turned down, though Debra Winger might have given it a go. Brand and Renn make an interesting couple in terms of their power balance. His instinct is to be the alpha male and to protect her, despite his habitual indifference to the pain of others, and the fact that she doesn't need his protection. But if you're going to get into torture porn and snuff movies, you have to mean it, and Nicki does. She is more hardcore than Renn the pornographer, who just likes to watch.

It would be a long time before David Cronenberg directed another film from his own original script. Now, he was about to step into the world of 'other people's material', and like one of his parasites, he would form a symbiotic relationship with the host.

The Dead Zone (1983)

Production: Dino De Laurentiis Corporation
Produced by Jeffrey Chernov, Dino De Laurentiis and Debra Hill
Written by Jeffrey Boam from the novel by Stephen King
Cinematographer: Mark Irwin
Music: Michael Kamen
Directed by David Cronenberg
Cast: Brooke Adams (Sarah Bracknell), Nicholas Campbell (Frank Dodd), Herbert Lom (Dr Sam Weizak), Martin Sheen (Greg Stillson), Tom Skerritt (Sheriff Bannerman), Christopher Walken (Johnny Smith)
Filming dates: 10 January to 26 March 1983
Canada release: 21 October 1983
US release: 21 October 1983
UK release: 13 January 1984
Running time: 103 minutes
Budget: $10 million

Background

Stanley Donen's *The Dead Zone*. Not quite the same as David Cronenberg's *The Dead Zone*. Soon after Stephen King's book was published in 1979, the veteran director and choreographer began working on an adaptation with screenwriter Jeffrey Boam, who producer Carol Baum at Lorimar had brought in. After Donen left the project and Lorimar closed its film division, Dino De Laurentiis came in but didn't like Boam's script. He asked Stephen King to write a draft, and he hired David Cronenberg to direct. King, who had just adapted his own stories for George A. Romero's *Creepshow*, turned in a screenplay that focused too heavily on the hunt for the Castle Rock killer. Cronenberg thought it needlessly brutal. King was out, and De Laurentiis hired another writer. When he rejected that script too, Dino returned to Jeffrey Boam.

Now Debra Hill joined as a producer to work with Cronenberg and Boam, and after a page-by-page revision, the screenplay was ready to go. Boam had thought of the story as a triptych suited to the usual three-act structure. For him, King's novel was too digressive to put all of it on screen. They cut out Johnny's brain tumour, so to speak. The serial killer storyline was clipped. A childhood incident during which injury gives Johnny his visions, was filmed but cut, as the car crash performs that function.

King would become a force in horror cinema, and had the best beginnings. *Carrie*, *'Salem's Lot* and *The Shining* were his three big adaptations so far. De Palma, Hooper and Kubrick: not bad. But King hated what Kubrick had done to his story.

Christopher Walken was not the only one up for the role of Johnny. Bill Murray, the choice of the novelist, had been considered first. Hal Holbrook would have been the sheriff if Cronenberg had got his way, but De Laurentiis said no.

Principal photography took place from January to March 1983, in and around the Toronto and Niagara areas, using landmarks for background colour, and creating a new one. A gazebo was built for the film in Queen's Royal Park, Niagara-on-the-Lake. Despite protests from locals, the town's officials agreed to its construction when Cronenberg assured them that it was temporary and could be torn down after the shoot. Instead, the production donated the gazebo to the town, where it has been a popular tourist attraction ever since.

A freeze had descended on Ontario, lasting many weeks, so the cast and crew had to work in almost intolerable sub-zero conditions. The upside was that the snow and ice gave the locations a frozen beauty, brought out by Mark Irwin's crisp cinematography.

This time, Howard Shore didn't compose. The studio wanted a more commercial name, so Michel Legrand was hired. He dropped out and was replaced at the last minute by Michael Kamen, whose sombre, dramatic, Sibelius-inspired music works marvellously and suits the film's intentions.

Story
In the pleasant burg of Castle Rock, Maine, where nothing remotely disturbing ever happens, a young teacher called Johnny Smith is reciting Poe's *The Raven* to his pupils. As the class ends, he asks them to read *Sleepy Hollow* for next time. They'll like it, he says, as it's a story in which a teacher is chased by a headless demon. Afterwards, in the corridor, he meets his colleague and fiancée Sarah Bracknell; they go out to enjoy an afternoon together. While they ride the rollercoaster at a fairground, Johnny is struck by a terrible headache. Driving home that night in his Beetle, he drops Sarah off despite her desire for him to spend the night. Soon it's raining heavily and visibility worsens. In the darkness, a truck loses its tank, which slides along the road until Johnny's car crashes into it and he blacks out.

Waking up in hospital, Johnny meets his neurologist, the kindly Doctor Weizak, who brings in the patient's parents, Vera and Herb. They tell Johnny that he's been in a coma for five years and that Sarah is now married. Johnny is heartbroken.

One day, as a nurse mops his brow, Johnny grabs her hand and receives a shocking vision of her daughter trapped in a burning house. He tells the nurse that Amy needs her and that it's not too late. Amy is saved from the fire, rescued by firefighters as her mother gets home.

Johnny begins rehabilitation under the care of Dr Weizak. After several weeks, he can walk again with the use of a cane. Taking the doctor's hand one time, Johnny has a sudden vision. He sees a small boy in a war, sent away to safety as his mother is left behind. When he comes out of the vision, Johnny tells Dr Weizak that his mother is alive. He also knows her name and where she lives.

The doctor goes out and finds his mother's house nearby, just where Johnny said it would be. He recognises her, now an elderly woman, but can't bring himself to say hello. He returns to Johnny and tells the young man that he has a gift. It's either a new human ability 'or a very old one'.

Sarah visits Johnny and reveals that she has a five-year-old son called Denny. She also tells him that the town is abuzz with stories of Johnny's visions.

Despite the doctor's advice, Johnny decides to hold a press conference to show the townsfolk that he's still a regular citizen. A reporter demands that Johnny demonstrate what he can do. Knowing he's being mocked, he takes the reporter's hand and asks the man if he wants to know why his sister killed herself.

Watching this at home, Johnny's mother Vera collapses and is brought to hospital, where he holds her hand while she passes away.

Johnny has moved in with his father Herb when the local sheriff comes to call. George Bannerman is desperate for help in solving a series of murders that have rocked the town. Johnny, wanting to be alone, refuses the request. Because Johnny considers his gift a curse, Herb angers him by suggesting that he should use his power to help others.

Sarah brings her son to visit Johnny, and in private, she and her old beau make love for one time only. As Sarah says, they've waited long enough.

Watching a TV report of the police investigation, Johnny changes his mind. He goes down to the crime scene, where he has a vision of who the killer is. It's Frank Dodd, Bannerman's deputy. Dodd kills himself rather than be arrested, then Dodd's mother shoots Johnny, and Bannerman shoots her dead.

Now further disabled and disillusioned, Johnny moves out of town to live a solitary life in a cabin, earning his living as a private tutor. His peace is disrupted when a rich man called Roger Stuart comes and begs him to see his son, Chris, who needs help. When Johnny has a vision of Chris and some other boys drowning after falling through the ice while playing hockey, Johnny tells Chris not to go out to the game. Stuart doesn't believe him, but Chris does and stays home. Two boys drown just as Johnny's vision showed, but Chris has been saved. Johnny now understands that his visions can change the future.

Sarah and her husband Walt volunteer on the campaign for a presidential candidate, Greg Stillson. Johnny joins them at a rally and in shaking Stillson's hand, receives a vision of the man in the Oval Office, ordering a pre-emptive nuclear strike against the Soviets, leading to all-out war. Billions will die.

Johnny goes to see Dr Weizak, asking his advice. If the doctor had met Hitler as a boy and knew what he would grow up to do, would he kill him? Weizak says that he would have no choice but to kill Hitler.

Resolved to act, Johnny leaves Sarah a letter telling her that he must do something which will result in his death.

Johnny brings a rifle to a rally for Stillson that is also attended by Sarah and her family. He shoots at the politician, and Stillson grabs Sarah's child, holding him up as a human shield. A press photographer captures this act of cowardice. Johnny's bullet has missed Stillson and before he can try again, a security guard shoots the would-be assassin. A furious Stillson comes over to Johnny, who takes his hand and sees one final vision. After the incriminating photograph appears in the press, Stillson's career will be over, and he will commit suicide, a broken man. Johnny tells him that he's finished, and after Stillson backs away, Sarah moves in to embrace the dying Johnny. She says she loves him.

Comment

Videodrome and *The Dead Zone* appeared in the same year. With one film, Cronenberg finally connected to the mainstream; with the other, he restated his manifesto of imagination.

The Dead Zone set his path as a director of adaptations, and a Stephen King novel was a good place to start. The story suited the director's need to grow; its emotional elements and fine characterisation were what he'd been looking for. Johnny Smith is sympathetic yet strange. He's not a hubristic scientist or an evil father figure. He's just a man, one of us but psychic. What matters in this story is the relationship between Johnny and Sarah. Lovers separated by time and a coma, they never really lose the spark between them but accept their changed roles in life. The implication that Sarah's child is also Johnny's, only adds to his tragedy. Johnny's empathy for those whose future he sees, necessarily drains him. Johnny is the ultimate introvert. Too much contact with people will leave him needing time alone.

Christopher Walken's unique acting style, its gentle oddity, is perfect for the role of Johnny.

Brooke Adams, famous for *Days of Heaven* (1977) and *Invasion of the Body Snatchers* (1978), is touching and resilient as Sarah, who still loves Johnny but has also found a good husband. Tom Skerrit as Sherriff Bannerman is decency personified. The scenes where Johnny and he work together to find the killer, are shocking and moving.

Johnny's answer to the Hitler conundrum is yes, partly out of moral necessity and partly because he knows that his visions are killing him. It's not revealed which party he belongs to, but Stillson resembles a comic-book version of Ronald Reagan. Martin Sheen, later of *The West Wing*, plays him as a terrifying, amoral opportunist who seeks power at all costs, a character who now looks rather prescient.

The Dead Zone ranks alongside *The Shining*, *Carrie*, *'Salem's Lot* and Frank Darabont's *The Mist* as the finest examples of King's horror in cinema. Cronenberg's first *bona fide* hit movie, critics received it warmly. Roger Ebert considered *The Dead Zone* the best King adaptation so far. The author himself agreed, reportedly telling Cronenberg that the film 'improved and intensified the power of the narrative'.

The Fly (1986)

Production: Brooksfilms
Produced by Marc-Ami Boyman, Stuart Cornfeld and Kip Ohman
Written by David Cronenberg and Charles Edward Pogue from the short story by George Langelaan
Cinematographer: Mark Irwin
Music by Howard Shore
Directed by David Cronenberg
Cast: Joy Boushel (Tawny), Les Carlson (Dr Cheevers), Geena Davis (Veronica Quaife), John Getz (Stathis Borans), Jeff Goldblum (Seth Brundle)
Filming dates: 1 December 1985 to 28 February 1986
US release: 15 August 1986
UK release: 13 February 1987
Running time: 96 minutes
Budget: $15 million

Background

A quarter of a century after the original film, co-producer Kip Ohman suggested a remake of *The Fly* to writer Charles Edward Pogue, who then worked with Stuart Cornfeld to pitch it to Fox. The studio liked the idea, and Pogue wrote a script, which they hated. Fox withdrew but later agreed to distribute the movie if it found funding elsewhere. Cornfeld took the project to Brooksfilms, who liked the script but felt it needed a new writer. In the game of musical chairs often played by screenwriters, Pogue was off the picture.

Mel Brooks, as well as making his own knockabout parodies, had been producing a run of prestige films by others, via his company Brooksfilms. The best of these was David Lynch's *The Elephant Man*. Now, Brooks and Cornfeld picked David Cronenberg for *The Fly*, but the director's commitment to *Total Recall* made him unavailable. In the meantime, they had hired another writer to rework Pogue's screenplay but had fired him too and brought Pogue back to do a polish.

Brooksfilms hired a young English director, Robert Bierman, but tragedy struck when his daughter died by accident on a family holiday. Naturally, Bierman left the picture to be with them. Mel Brooks gave him three months off to grieve and to think about whether he wanted to continue with *The Fly*. A compassionate move; another studio might have dropped Bierman. When he decided he couldn't do the film, Brooks amicably released him from his contract. Robert Bierman went on to have a successful career in film and television, including an excellent adaptation of Orwell's *Keep the Aspidistra Flying* (1997).

By the time David Cronenberg had done with *Total Recall*, *The Fly* was again in need of a director. Brooksfilms came back to him and he agreed to do the picture if he could rewrite the script. He got more than that. Mel Brooks told him to go as far as he needed to make the film he wanted to make.

The screenplay grew from the scaffolding of Pogue's story and used some of his ideas. Cronenberg added his own and made some crucial changes. Instead of having the protagonist turn into a giant fly (closer to the old movie), his story merged man and fly into something new. Cronenberg, who had built on the other man's work, insisted on a writing credit for Pogue.

The Fly was the last film Mark Irwin shot for the director, and he goes out on a high. The movie looks terrific, which sometimes means terrifically gross and beautiful at the same time.

Chris Walas and Stephan Dupuis created the special make-up effects, for which they deservedly won an Oscar. Walas would go on to direct *The Fly II*.

The casting of Geena Davis and Jeff Goldblum gave the audience sympathetic characters to root for as the horror unfolded, helping *The Fly* to spike the mainstream with Cronenberg's signature obsessions. Once again, he'd courted the general moviegoing public without having to compromise.

Story

At a press launch, science journalist Veronica Quaife meets Seth Brundle, an eccentric genius who is working on a major project, funded by Bartok Industries. Suggesting he might give her an exclusive story, Brundle takes 'Ronnie' back to his laboratory, where he also lives, in a loft-style warehouse. It looks like a cleaner hasn't seen the place for years.

Brundle's invention is startling: teleport. He has built a pair of chambers, telepods, between which a person might be transported instantly. Except he hasn't got it to work on organic matter, not yet. It does unfortunate things to a steak, transporting the molecules but reassembling them in a different order. The steak when cooked still tastes like meat but there's something off about it. Brundle promises Ronnie the exclusive rights to his teleport story if she agrees to keep it secret for now.

An experimental attempt to transmit a living creature goes wrong when Seth teleports a baboon from one pod to the other. The baboon arrives inverted, its innards on the outside, its suffering horrendous.

Having agreed to write the story, Ronnie begins a relationship with Seth. After they have sex, he gets an idea. He reprograms the teleport computer to understand living tissue. This time he succeeds, teleporting a second baboon without harming it.

A breakthrough, but Ronnie leaves before they can celebrate. Stathis Borans, her editor at the magazine, has threatened to publish the Brundle article prematurely, without her permission. Borans, Ronnie's ex-lover, is jealous of her and Seth. She has gone to challenge him, but Brundle thinks she wants to get back with her old flame.

Self-pitying and drinking, Brundle impulsively decides to teleport himself. Without his knowledge, a housefly enters the telepod with him. Brundle emerges from the other pod apparently unaffected.

Ronnie has given Borans a piece of her mind and convinced Seth that the man is no threat. As she and Brundle continue their relationship, his body begins to change. He's stronger, fitter and his sexual appetite increases. Brundle reasons that these improvements must be down to a purifying effect of the teleportation process. He's been cleansed and made new. But there's something not right with all this. He starts to crave sugar. Strange bristles poke out of his back. He is becoming more manic and impulsive. Ronnie is worried about what is happening to Seth, but he refuses to admit there's a problem. When she tries to talk with him about her concerns, he turns nasty, insisting that she must also go through the teleporter. Ronnie refuses, and he goes out into the night.

At a dive bar, Brundle gets into an arm-wrestling contest, intending to test his new strength. He wins easily but violently, giving the other man a compound fracture. Before anyone can challenge Brundle, he hooks up with a woman, Tawny, and takes her back to his laboratory. She and Brundle have sex, which turns rough and frightening. He tries to get her to teleport. Ronnie arrives into the room and saves Tawny, warning her to leave. Seth, in turn, makes Ronnie go.

Left on his own, Brundle, the scientist begins to observe the process of change in his body and mind. His fingernails start to fall off, making him realise that something went wrong in the teleport. The answer must be in the computer, so Brundle checks the record and finds out there were two lifeforms in the machine when he went through. Not knowing how to process them both, the telepod fused their molecules into a new form of life.

Over the following weeks, Seth continues to lose parts of his human self as more fly-like elements assert themselves, his hybrid nature more pronounced. Finally, he is too afraid to be alone, and he calls Ronnie, telling her what is happening. He now has a name for what he is: Brundlefly, a creature that can cling to walls and jump across ceilings, and which vomits enzymes on its food before slurping it back up. Brundle needs Ronnie to stay with him, but the fly is submerging his humanity, burying his empathy. He can't control the darker impulses that push to the surface. Hoping that some of his human identity will survive, he declares his interest in being the first insect politician.

Seth has an idea of how to save himself. He sets a fusion program in the computer and instructs it to dilute the fly DNA with his human material. He goes through the telepod again, but the program doesn't work. The fly will not be diminished.

A horrified Ronnie learns that she is pregnant, and after a nightmare in which she gives birth to a giant maggot, she knows that she carries the offspring of Brundlefly. She goes to Borans, who agrees to arrange an emergency abortion for her, but Brundle has been eavesdropping, and he follows them to the clinic.

Before the procedure can be carried out, Brundle bursts into the surgery room, horrifying Borans and the doctor, and kidnapping Ronnie. He takes her back to his lab and implores her to go full term with the foetus. It may be the only hope for his human side.

Stathis Borans breaks in, carrying a shotgun, but Seth vomits acid on the man's leg and disables him. Now Seth reveals his plans. He will fuse himself, Ronnie and her foetus using the telepods, to create a single lifeform that's free of impurities. He pulls Ronnie towards the pod, but she tears off his jaw and he staggers back, wholly Brundlefly, discarding the remains of Seth's human body. Brundlefly locks Ronnie into one telepod then enters the other.

Borans, rallying though wounded, shoots the cable connecting the computer to Ronnie's telepod. She is released, but Seth is trapped as the fusion begins. Having nothing human to splice with him, the computer merges him with the telepod itself. As this happens, Brundle-pod crawls away from the wreckage and looks up at Ronnie with imploring eyes, a suffering consciousness within this hideous form. Ronnie holds Borans's shotgun, and the creature lifts the barrel to its forehead. With tears in her eyes, Ronnie pulls the trigger and puts Seth Brundle out of his misery.

Comment

The Fly is in part based on a story by George Langelaan, published in the June 1957 issue of *Playboy*. The story inspired a trilogy of films at the time, of which the original is still the best remembered, for its ridiculous yet strangely moving ending. Cronenberg uses the story's premise to pursue his own concerns: disease, the merging of technology with biology, and metamorphosis via creative destruction.

His film is an allegory of disease, if not exactly of the AIDS pandemic, then new to cinema in the form of a mention in Woody Allen's *Hannah and Her Sisters*. It is also a great romance between two different kinds of creatures, as the director might say; and a love story played out with actors whose real-life attraction illuminated their performances. Geena Davis is excellent as Ronnie, who finds the strength to protect herself from her increasingly toxic boyfriend. Goldblum is perfect for Brundle, endowing the scientist with just the right amount of eccentricity and geeky charm. You just know these characters understand each other. Borans, wittily played by John Getz, at first comes over as a standard evil ex, then turns out to be Ronnie's saviour, helping her to arrange an abortion. His motives may be impure, but he's just what she needs at that point. Interrupted though the procedure is, no one except the father is seriously proposing that Ronnie should go through with the pregnancy. You could see this story as a feminist warning about toxic masculinity, but if it was Ronnie who merged with the fly, she would have been no less intent on reproduction. Beyond such considerations, here is a genuinely emotional experience, making us feel sympathy for a monster and the man he used to be, as well as for the damaged humans he leaves in his wake of destruction. It's also a touching love story in the tradition of *Beauty and the Beast*, *The Phantom of the Opera*, and *The Incredible Shrinking Man*. From the perspective of 35 years, it is clear that the film's power has not diminished. *The Fly* has become a classic of its genre, not to mention quite simply a classic of cinema in general.

Dead Ringers (1988)

Production: The Mantle Clinic II, Ltd., Morgan Creek Productions, Inc., Telefilm Canada
Produced by Carol Baum, John Board, Marc Boyman, David Cronenberg, James G. Robinson, Joe Roth and Sylvio Tabet
Written by David Cronenberg and Norman Snider from the book *Twins* by Bari Wood and Jack Geasland
Cinematographer: Peter Suschitzky
Music: Howard Shore
Optical Effects Designer: Lee Wilson
Directed by David Cronenberg
Filming dates: 1 February 1988 to 12 April 1988
Canada release: 8 September 1988
US release: 23 September 1988
UK release: 6 January 1989
Running time: 115 minutes
Budget: $10-11 million
Cast: Geneviève Bujold (Claire Niveau), Barbara Gordon (Danuta), Jeremy Irons (Beverly Mantle, Elliot Mantle), Stephen Lack (Anders Wolleck), Heidi von Palleske (Cary Weiler)

Background

Buoyed by the success of *The Fly*, David Cronenberg resumed a project he had begun developing in 1980, when he and two producers optioned *Twins* by Bari Wood and Jack Geasland. The novel, published in 1977, is a fictional account of a real case. Twin-brother gynaecologists Stewart and Cyril Marcus were found decomposing in their New York apartment, having died four days apart of either barbiturate overdoses or withdrawal symptoms. What happened during those four days? Thereby hangs a shocking tale.

The film changes the setting to Toronto, as Cronenberg and co-writer Norman Snider set out to develop a 'non-adaptation'. Their screenplay separates the movie from the book with surgical precision, but they credit Wood and Geasland, if only to rule out any potential legal issues with the Marcus estate.

It wasn't even an adaptation in name only. The filmmakers settled on *Dead Ringers* as the title when Ivan Reitman called his new comedy *Twins*. *Dead Ringers* works better, its pulp-ish glamour setting the film's operatic decadence in relief, and connoting the kind of horror you don't get from the word 'twins' unless you follow it with 'of' and 'evil'.

The cast could have been different. Due to a scheduling conflict, William Hurt, the director's first choice for the Mantles, had to turn the film down. Uncomfortable with the idea of playing a gynaecologist, let alone two, Robert De Niro also said no. In the end, Jeremy Irons was cast. He used the Alexander technique to give each twin a distinctive energy, carriage and poise.

Geneviève Bujold, a national treasure in Canada, played Claire Niveau, who helps divide the twins. Margot Kidder had been considered. In supporting roles, Heidi von Palleske, Stephen Lack and Barbara Gordon are excellent. Jill and Jacqueline Hennessy, twin sisters, make their film debuts here, playing the escorts that Elliot summons to his hotel room.

Photography began on 1 February 1988 at various locations around Toronto and lasted for eleven weeks, shot by Peter Suschitzky.

Lee Wilson, the optical effects supervisor, used a new technique to place both Mantles on screen at once, creating the 'twinning' shots on set. One half of the picture was filmed with a locked-off camera or a motion-control dolly as required. This was fed back to a monitor where a split-screen allowed for the second half to be framed, lit and shot to match. For decades, films would hide such a split using elements of the set, such as a door or a wall, to make a vertical match. *Dead Ringers* does something subtler and more complex, combining the split-screen with camera movement. Fourteen shots were done this way, and they work so well that you don't notice the join, you just marvel at the achievement.

Doppelganger comedy *Big Business* came out a few months before *Dead Ringers* and used a similar effect, but it's the latter film that technically got there first, and which people remember.

Also memorable are the film's 'surgical instruments for operating on mutant women'. The production design team led by Carol Spier developed these beauties, inspired by real surgical tools, dental instruments, dildos, bones, and parts of the body. One of the instruments mimics the female reproductive system, another a talon, and another resembles a pelvis. One of them recalls the parasite that rapes Betts in *Shivers*. Art director Peter Grundy made sketches of the instruments to guide a jewellery designer hired to produce these objects. The results are impeccable and effective. Who wouldn't have nightmares about such invasive, not to mention sharp, objects?

When *Dead Ringers* came out in September 1988, the response was positive, if qualified. Roger Ebert reported: 'I saw it at the Toronto Film Festival with several women friends, who said it was harder for them to take than I, a man, could possibly imagine. But they were fascinated while it was on the screen.'

Irons was named Best Actor at the NY Film Critics Circle awards. He should have won for Best Supporting Actor too. Bujold was recognised for both this and Alan Rudolph's *The Moderns* at the LA Film Critics Association, which also named David Cronenberg Best Director. In Canada, the film won ten Genies, including awards for Shore and Suschitzky. In 2015, the last time the Toronto International Film Festival compiled its list of Top 10 Canadian Films of All Time, *Dead Ringers* was at number seven. The film is now a classic, even if it is still not for the squeamish.

Story

Toronto, 1954. Two nine-year-old identical twins, Beverly and Elliot Mantle, walk down the street, discussing reproduction. The only reason humans have sex, they reason, is because humans don't live underwater but must 'internalise' it. Precocious and strangely detached, they ask a young girl they meet if she will have sex with them in a bath, to test their theory. She tells them to 'fuck off'. Back at home, the boys play dispassionately with a gynaecological model.

Cambridge, Massachusetts, 1967. The twins excel in their medical studies while showing interest in unorthodox methods. They win a prize for inventing a gynaecological instrument known as the Mantle retractor, which becomes the industry standard.

A couple of decades later, the boys have grown up to be celebrated gynaecologists with their own successful practice in the city, the Mantle Clinic, in which they also have their luxurious living quarters.

For some time now Elliot and Beverly have been sharing women, in work and in play. Romantically, 'Ellie' passes them on to 'Bev', his 'baby brother', when he himself has tired of them. It's assumed that the women don't detect the switch, as outgoing Elliot pretends to be the introverted Beverly. However, one of their girlfriends, Dr Cary Weiler, is so in tune with them that she can sense the difference intuitively.

When a famous actress, Claire Niveau, attends the clinic, Beverly finds that she has a trifurcated cervix, and will never have children. He asks Elliot to look, and they swap places in the surgery, unbeknownst to the patient. Elliot is quite impressed by this discovery and fails to empathise with Claire's plight. Elliot starts an affair with her then urges Beverly to take over. Beverly becomes infatuated and begins a relationship with the actress. Emotional involvement was never the plan, as far as Elliot is concerned, so when Beverly gets ever more attached to Claire, the bond between the brothers comes under strain.

Claire is a drug addict, which she sees as an occupational hazard, and she makes Beverly complicit by getting him to write prescriptions for her. As a result, he forms a habit of his own. Helping her read a part one day, Beverly lets his guard down. Claire asks him if he'd ever done impressions as a child, and he replies, 'only my brother'. They argue, as she didn't realise he had a brother, and she accuses him of having a girl's name. They take drugs to restore their equilibrium.

At lunch one day, a friend asks Claire which of the Mantle boys she's dating, and tells her that no one can tell the twins apart. Claire realises that Elliot has been impersonating Beverly and that she has been sleeping with both men.

She invites the Mantles to meet her in a restaurant, where she confronts them angrily for having deceived her. Then she storms off after Elliot proves not only unapologetic but sarcastic, insulting her and leaving Beverly upset.

Sometime later, when Elliot is giving an acceptance speech for an award in their honour, Beverly pipes up and drunkenly interrupts his brother. Elliot has told the audience that Beverly is at home, working. Bev staggers to the podium and demands to make a speech. His resentment is clear as he tells the room that he does all the work while Elliot takes all the glory, but not in those words. Elliot takes over and tells the audience that Beverly has been doing a little celebrating after all, and who can blame him? He and Cary take Beverly home.

A few feathers were ruffled by this incident, but not seriously. The next day, Elliot tells Beverly that he has accepted a professorship, so Bev will have to run the clinic in his absence.

While Elliot is away, Beverly descends further into drug addiction, lost without his brother, and mooning over his sabotaged love affair. Then he meets Claire by chance and she cautiously agrees to restart their relationship. Perhaps she needs someone to write prescriptions for her; she's cooler with him than before.

One night, while sleeping with Claire, Beverly has a terrible nightmare. He sees Elliot in the bed beside him. The brothers are joined at the chest by a mass of flesh and skin, as though grafted on each other. Claire bites through the connecting tissue, separating the twins. Beverly wakes up in a cold sweat.

Elliot, on an academic tour, is waiting in a hotel room when his order arrives: a pair of identical twin escorts, young and beautiful. He asks one of them to call him 'Ellie' and the other to call him 'Bev'.

Back at the Mantle clinic, Beverly's condition deteriorates. His hands shake while he operates on a patient. His drug-taking worsens to the extent that he has Claire call Danuta, the clinic's secretary, to cancel his appointments.

Before she leaves the city to work on a film shoot, Claire calls Elliot to her trailer, because she's worried that Beverly will be alone and vulnerable when she's gone. Elliot, back from his tour, counters that Beverly is never alone, but Claire disagrees. Even when she and Bev are together, he is still alone. Elliot's solution is for the three of them to have a relationship. Claire turns that down, as, to her, the two brothers are so different, an observation that seems to surprise Elliot. They agree a truce. She wants him to take care of Beverly when she's away.

Claire's concern is proven right. Without her, Beverly descends into a clinical depression. He calls her hotel and Claire's gay male secretary answers the phone. Beverly scandalises the man with an insult, convinced that Claire is being unfaithful with him. In the apartment, a tearful Beverly confides this to Elliot, who is dancing with Cary. Elliot asks Beverly to join them. The three dance together to the Five Satins. Beverly collapses, Elliot revives him then gets an ambulance to take him to hospital.

Elliot tries to cover for Beverly while getting him clean. But as his drug use intensifies, Beverly becomes convinced that his patients' reproductive organs are abnormal. When he returns to work, Bev injures a patient but insists that it's her fault. He tells a worried Elliot that the instruments were fine; it was the woman's body that was wrong. Bev commissions a sculptor, Wolleck, to produce a set of gynaecological instruments for operating on mutant women. Thinking it an art project, Wolleck makes a set of unusual and terrifying objects in surgical steel, to Beverly's specifications.

When she finds Bev injecting drugs in the surgery, Danuta resigns, leaving the brothers alone together at last.

During an operation, Bev uses one of Wolleck's instruments on a patient and wounds her. His colleagues in theatre, appalled, remove him urgently.

The Mantles are called before a disciplinary board, which suspends them, and their careers as practising gynaecologists are over.

Cary believes Elliot should drop his brother and save his own career, but Elliot can't do that. He tells her the story of Siamese twins, Chang and Eng. When one had a stroke and died, the other twin, waking up to find his brother deceased, expired of sheer fright.

Elliot makes a decision. He will take the same drugs that Beverly is taking, and they will synchronise their states of mind. Perhaps then they can help each other.

Claire returns from the shoot and calls Bev to come over. On the way, he passes Wolleck's gallery and sees a set of his mutant instruments on display. He steals them, much to the sculptor's consternation.

At Claire's apartment, he writes a prescription for a hypnotic drug. They spend a week together and he seems to improve as time passes. However, he hasn't heard from Elliot. Beverly goes to the clinic where he finds Elliot in a worse state than his own.

Finally becoming the grown-up brother, Beverly decides to stay and help Ellie recover. They agree to synchronise their drug intake then go cold turkey simultaneously. Deciding it's their birthday, they celebrate with pills, cake and orange pop. Beverly recalls once more the story of Chang and Eng. Then, with Elliot's consent, he uses the Wolleck sculptures to separate the Siamese twins: themselves. Beverly injects Elliot with a sedative before cutting his brother's wrist open with a mutant instrument shaped like a bony finger. Everything is required, they agree.

Days pass. Beverly wakes up from a terrible dream. He calls out to Elliot as he walks around the apartment: 'Ellie...Ellie...'. Realising it's not a dream and that he has killed his brother, Beverly shaves, puts on a clean suit and shirt, and goes out with his suitcase to phone Claire from the booth in the square. She answers, 'Who is this?' Beverly leaves his case in the booth and returns to the apartment.

Now we see a final tableau in the Mantle clinic. Pale Elliot drained of blood, a corpse on the examination couch. Beverly's body settled in front of him, the twins separated at last but together forever in death.

Comment

In his subtle, intelligent performance, Jeremy Irons embodies each of the Mantle twins completely and distinctly, and the viewer gets a clear sense of Elliot and Beverly's contrasting personalities. The actor excels at portraying the detachment that they feel from ordinary humans and ambivalently wish to achieve from each other.

Although he started with a dressing room for each character, Irons soon decided to use one for both, a choice that makes sense. Two bodies, one mind.

The film looks and sounds exquisite. Howard Shore composes a dark orchestral conjuring of the characters' inner demons. Strangely romantic with a lower-case 'r', it is Shore's saddest and most beautiful work for this director. With his delicate, fine-art style, Peter Suschitzky elevates *Dead Ringers* as Cronenberg's first painterly film.

The psychological insights are the director's deepest yet, with a sense of dark fairytale about the story of the Mantles that hits close to home for anyone who knows what it means to be codependent.

One of Cronenberg's abiding interests is the nature of identity, and this film's exploration of duality harks back to his earliest work. What if two bodies share the same mind? In attempting to answer that question, he takes a comparatively low-key approach. Despite the dream sequence with its gristle, *Dead Ringers* feels philosophical and melancholy. There is no need for a parasite when the story is about what needs to come out rather than what might get in.

Irons and Bujold spark off each other, whichever twin is in the frame, but especially in the scenes between Beverly and Claire. He needs her more than she needs him, as he finally gets to have something for himself. It is this need, fed by her desire to smother her own pain with the love and medication he supplies, that threatens the bond between the brothers.

The actors sell this despair with a naked grace, especially when the film turns away from Beverly and Claire to focus on the brothers' final descent. One could wish for more of Bujold in *Dead Ringers*, but as Bev and Ellie's world closes in, hermetically sealing their fate, there is no room for Claire. This feels truthful.

For all the emotional restraint in the film, a feeling of hurt burns behind its surgical-steel exterior. The devastated twins have themselves to blame and only each other to believe in. If they would let a little kindness in, a little light, they might survive. But there is no space between them, which is why their final separation is so affecting. There is beauty in the pain of these conjoined souls, and death is what freedom demands. For the Mantle boys to separate, everything is required.

Naked Lunch (1991)

Production: Recorded Picture Company
Distribution: 20ᵗʰ Century Fox
Produced by Jeremy Thomas, Gabriella Martinelli
Written by David Cronenberg based on the novel by William Burroughs
Cinematographer: Peter Suschitzky
Music: Howard Shore, Ornette Coleman
Directed by David Cronenberg
Filming: January–April 1991
US release: 27 December 1991 (limited)
UK release: 12 December 1991 (premiere), 24 April 1992 (general)
Running time: 115 minutes
Budget: $17–18 million
Cast: Judy Davis (Joan Frost, Joan Lee), Ian Holm (Tom Frost), Monique Mercure (Fadele), Julian Sands (Yves Cloquet), Roy Scheider (Dr Benway), Joseph Scorsiani (Kiki), Peter Weller (William Lee)

Background

Published as *The Naked Lunch* by the Olympia Press, Paris, in 1959, William Burroughs' book is among the key texts of the Beat movement, its title suggested by Jack Kerouac. Having been delayed by American obscenity laws, the novel appeared in the US from Grove Press in 1962. This edition differs from the Olympia in that it uses an earlier manuscript held by Allen Ginsberg, and its title drops the definite article. The book anticipated AIDS, liposuction and auto-erotic asphyxiation while making one of the great leaps forward in the evolution of the novel. Like Joyce before him with *Finnegans Wake*, Burroughs takes scissors to the idea of the novel itself, then puts it back together as a kind of free-form jazz.

David Cronenberg, studying literature in the early 1960s, was influenced by Burroughs, and many years later surprised himself by telling an interviewer that he'd like to film *Naked Lunch*.

Others had tried. In 1970, with Burroughs' blessing, his friends Brion Gysin and Antony Baich attempted to adapt the book. Gysin wrote a script that included music-hall comedy songs. After four years without success, despite their desire to have Mick Jagger star as Bill Lee, development stopped.

Then in 1979, Frank Zappa approached Burroughs with the idea of making an off-Broadway musical of the novel. This intrigued the author, but the musical wasn't made.

In February 1984, Burroughs met Cronenberg for the first time, in New York. Burroughs hadn't seen the director's films, but when he did, their admiration became mutual.

As reported in Ira Silverberg's *Everything is Permitted: The Making of Naked Lunch*, producer Jeremy Thomas came up to Cronenberg at TIFF later that year, saying that he'd heard of his interest in the novel, a film of which Thomas was 'dying to produce'. He asked if Cronenberg knew Burroughs.

So began a journey to Interzone. In 1985, a party that included Thomas, Cronenberg and Burroughs, travelled to Tangier. On his first trip back since 1972, Burroughs noted the changes and saw that his friend Paul Bowles still lived there. Bowles would play a cameo as himself, in Bertolucci's *The Sheltering Sky* (1990), also produced by Jeremy Thomas.

Over the next five years, Cronenberg and Burroughs met a number of times without a word of the screenplay being written, and they discussed many questions, none directly related to what kind of film version Burroughs would like to see.

Cronenberg later said he had needed the 'spirit' of Burroughs to 'quietly possess' him. When he realised that his job was to 'translate' the material, he found a way in: instead of bringing Burroughs across into his world, Cronenberg immersed himself in the realm of the author, blending parts of *Naked Lunch*, *Queer*, *Exterminator!*, and aspects of Burroughs' own life story.

During a three-month stay in London, while acting in Clive Barker's *Nightbreed*, Cronenberg found himself writing his screenplay for *Naked Lunch*. The story flowed out of him like automatic writing. By the end, he felt so in tune with the author, the sympathy between them so strong, that should Burroughs die, he would 'just write his next book'.

Deciding against using the names of real drugs, Cronenberg presented a fair representation of what it is like to take them. The black meat, bug powder and Mugwump jism? All part of the hallucination.

Peter Weller, who says that he read *Naked Lunch* once a year, was cast as William Lee. He didn't need much persuasion. Speaking to an audience after a screening of *Robocop* in 2013, he said 'I begged Cronenberg to do *Naked Lunch*. I grew up with *Naked Lunch* ... I'm a child of the sixties ...' Known to cult audiences for his role as Buckaroo Banzai, Weller was no stranger to idiosyncratic projects.

Judy Davis, who plays Joan and her avatars, was known for *My Brilliant Career* (1979) and *A Passage to India* (1984). Ian Holm, in his first film with Cronenberg, is Tom Frost, Joan's *other* husband. Together they play a fictional version of Paul and Jane Bowles.

When it looked like Cronenberg would film *Naked Lunch* outside Canada, the Ontario Film Board offered funding and incentives to keep it in the country. They needn't have, as the first Iraq invasion prevented travel to Morocco. Carol Spier and her team recreated Tangier on a soundstage in a Toronto munitions factory. They used seven hundred tons of sand for the indoor desert, and an array of translight photographs to create the backgrounds, giving the film a certain artificiality that works in its favour.

Since *The Fly*, David Cronenberg's title sequences had been designed to set the scene. Those of *Naked Lunch* were crafted in homage to Saul Bass, evoking the period in which the story is set. As well as music by Howard Shore, the bebop-inspired score features 'Midnight Sunrise' by Ornette Coleman, the

1973 recording of which Burroughs attended. Contributions from the Master Musicians of Joujouka complete the aural journey back in time.

Naked Lunch had a limited release in the US, with little commercial success. Some critics admired it; others found it flat. Janet Maslin at the *New York Times* called it 'coolly riveting and darkly entertaining', but Vanessa Letts at the *Spectator* was unimpressed, blaming Cronenberg who 'has taken credit for this adaptation'. 'In fact,' Letts says, 'some of the best moments in the film come when Burroughs is simply recited verbatim ... the talking asshole is funnier as a story than as a bit of latex cinematic wizardry'. Weller won a Genie Award for Best Performance by a Leading Actor.

The film's stature has grown with time, and *Naked Lunch* is regarded as one of the best films about writing. *Cinephilia and Beyond* said, '*Naked Lunch* might not be everybody's cup of tea, but it's an exotic tea we like to enjoy whenever we feel the world has become perhaps a bit too ordinary'.

Story

Exterminator Bill Lee is spraying for bugs in a New York apartment when he runs out of bug powder. His boss isn't happy. This stuff isn't cheap.

Bill meets two friends, Martin and Hank, in a bar. They're writers, discussing the craft. One of them believes in rewriting, the other disagrees, as it's a form of self-censorship. Bill has given up writing because he views it as too dangerous. 'Exterminate all rational thought' is his writing advice.

When he gets home, he finds his wife Joan shooting up his bug powder. So that's why he's been running out. She tells him it's a 'Kafka high' and he should inject it too.

Later, Lee is arrested for possession of banned substances. The narcs put him in a room with a monstrously large beetle that is eating bug powder. The bug asks Lee to rub the powder into its asshole, then introduces itself as his case officer. It gives Bill a task: he must kill Joan, for she is not human, but an agent of Interzone Inc. Lee steps on the bug, killing it, and gets out of there.

Back home he admits to Joan that he is hallucinating and was arrested for using bug powder.

At work, a colleague gives Lee the card of Doctor Benway, who can cure him. Benway gives him 'black centipede powder' to counter the original drug. On the way home, Lee sees a stall selling enormous centipedes for meat. This makes him feel sick. Back home, he finds Joan having sex with Hank while Martin speaks beat poetry. Lee injects himself and his wife with bug powder then says it's time for their 'William Tell routine'. Joan agrees and puts a drinking glass on her head. Lee shoots but misses the glass. A bloody hole appears in Joan's forehead and she collapses, dead.

Lee goes to a bar where he meets a Mugwump, an alien that advises him to bring a Clark-Nova typewriter to Interzone, where he can type up the report of Joan's death. The Mugwump gives him a ticket for the trip.

Pawning his gun in exchange for the typewriter, Lee goes to Interzone, a

Tangier-like city on the coast of North Africa, a meeting point of many cultures, an in-between state.

In Interzone, Lee meets a drug manufacturer called Hans, who owns the factory that makes black centipede meat. Bill finds himself in his room talking with the Clark-Nova, which transforms into a beetle-typewriter hybrid and tells Lee that homosexuality is an ideal cover for an agent.

Lee now meets two American writers at a social event: Tom and Joan Frost. Joan is a doppelganger of Lee's dead wife, whose maiden name was Frost. Telepathically, Tom tells Lee that he himself is killing his own wife, employing the housekeeper to do so. After leaving the party, Lee wakes up on the beach, where a socialite, Cloquet, comes to collect him. Because Cloquet approves of Lee, Tom Frost lends him his own typewriter, a Martinelli. Lee takes the Martinelli home.

As he sleeps, the Clark-Nova kills the interloper, the commotion waking him. The Clark-Nova says that the Martinelli is an agent for the other side and that Lee should seduce Joan Frost to find out what she knows.

Lee visits Joan and tells her he's destroyed the Martinelli. Joan says that they have another typewriter, an Arabic machine. It's called a Mujahedin. Joan types on it and the machine becomes organic, a vagina opening in its flesh. As Bill caresses her, Joan puts her fingers into the typewriter's vagina, then while the two humans make love, the creature jumps up on them and joins in, humping away.

The housekeeper interrupts, flinging the bug-writer out across the balcony and onto the street below, where it changes back into a typewriter, smashed. Lee and Joan follow the housekeeper, Fadela, to the casbah, where she is selling centipede meat.

At home, the Clark-Nova tells Lee that he was programmed to kill his wife, who was an elite centipede. Tom walks in, furious that Lee destroyed his Martinelli; he leaves the broken machine and takes the Clark-Nova as compensation.

Back on the beach, Martin and Hank find Lee, and they tell him to finish his book, chapters from which he has been sending them. The book is called *Naked Lunch*. Bill is mystified.

With the help of Cloquet's friend Kiki, Lee brings the Martinelli to a forge, where it is remade as a typewriter with a Mugwump head. This machine tells him that Doctor Benway is the mastermind of Interzone Inc., and he runs the market for centipede meat. As Lee and Kiki ride in Cloquet's car, Lee tells a story of a man who taught his asshole to talk. The asshole soon developed the desire to have its own, independent life.

At Cloquet's house, Bill follows him and Kiki when they go into the bedroom. Cloquet has turned into a giant insect which is consuming Kiki's body.

Leaving them, Bill takes the Mugwump-writer to Tom Frost to exchange it for the Clark-Nova. However, the Nova is dying, having been tortured. Before it expires, it tells Lee that Interzone is to be found in Hans' factory.

The factory has changed. Mugwumps are now hung up like cattle to be milked for their addictive jism. Fadela is here, and pulling her own skin off, reveals that she is in fact Benway with an offer for Lee, who accepts on one condition. He will go to Annexia as an agent for Benway but only if he can bring Joan Frost.

Arriving at the border in an unusual truck, Lee drives while Joan sleeps on the passenger seat. Lee has to prove to the guards that he's a writer, so he wakes Joan, telling her it's time for their William Tell routine. Joan puts a drinking glass on her head and Lee shoots her. Distraught, he cries softly as the guard welcomes him to Annexia.

Comment

In a 1996 episode of *The Simpsons*, Bart and friends use a fake ID to see *Naked Lunch* at a movie theatre. Afterwards, one of them remarks, 'I can think of at least two things wrong with that title'. A critic might say that what was 'wrong' with the title was obvious. The film wasn't quite *Naked Lunch*. It was more. Cronenberg attempted the impossible by not attempting the impossible. Rather than make a direct adaptation – that $400,000,000 banned masterpiece – he took from the novel what he needed, mixed in elements of biography, and seasoned the script with material from the writer's other work. The 'lunch' he serves up is a metafictional mezze and all the richer for that.

Today, the book could be filmed intact by using CGI, but ironically the 'uncanny valley' effect would undermine its power. Cronenberg's film feels tactile, febrile, a handmade horror, and a clever meditation on the nature of the creative writing process. The performances are great. Weller brings an icy charisma to Lee. Davis, as the Joans, shares a sense of recklessness with the audience. Holm is excellent as Frost, a believably boozy writer with an open-minded attitude to most things. And Roy Scheider presents a flamboyant Benway.

The story of *Naked Lunch* begins in the real world with the death of Joan Vollmer, William Burroughs' second wife, in 1951, during their time in Mexico. According to different accounts the author gave, Joan died either when he shot her during a 'William Tell routine' while they were both intoxicated and high, or when his pistol went off accidentally as he was showing it to friends. In the preface to his book *Queer*, Burroughs acknowledged the 'appalling conclusion' that he would never have been a writer were it not for this event. He believed that Joan's death had opened him up to literal possession by an 'ugly spirit'. Burroughs skipped Mexico and was convicted in absentia, of manslaughter. He was sentenced to two years, suspended. Contrary to his view that Joan's death made him a writer, he had already nearly completed *Junkie* and had written a collaborative book with Kerouac in 1945. Rather, his guilt for the crime shaped the kind of writer he would be. Two years later, Burroughs, inspired by Bowles, went to Tangier International Zone, the real-life Interzone, where writing became his way of fending off the incoming demons.

Joan's killing becomes a recurring image in Cronenberg's film, its repetition calling out the darkness Bill Lee lives in, the awful knowledge of what he has done, the well of pain from which he draws for his art. The theme is again creative destruction, in this case, the price an artist pays and, as often happens, the suffering inflicted on innocent civilians. Art is not a victimless crime.

Naked Lunch moves from one act of destruction to the next. When he kills Joan, Lee has to jump into his subconscious to find her again. She may be his Ariadne, but he is here to sacrifice himself to the Minotaur. Meanwhile, he is getting all this down, just like a writer. Typing the story of his pain on a machine that talks through its asshole and also has wings, your standard insect-keyboard-warrior, Bill Lee is, in fact, writing the novel that will be called *Naked Lunch*.

'Exterminate all rational thought', the slogan, is our most useful guide to the film. Like Number Six in *The Prisoner* (1967), Lee can never leave his weird and terrifying nowhere-place because he controls it. He created this half-world, and you cannot escape a prison that you build around yourself. William Burroughs knew this. *Naked Lunch*, the novel, is the note he smuggled out.

M. Butterfly (1993)

Production: Geffen Pictures
Produced by David Henry Hwang, Gabriella Martinelli, and Philip Sandhaus
Written by David Henry Hwang from his play
Cinematographer: Peter Suschitzky
Music by Howard Shore
Directed by David Cronenberg
Filming dates: August to December 1992
Canada release: 9 September 1993 (TIFF)
US release: 1 October 1993
UK release: 6 May 1994
Running time: 101 minutes
Budget:
Cast: Shizuko Hoshi (Comrade Chin), Jeremy Irons (René Gallimard), Annabel
Leventon (Frau Baden), John Lone (Song Liling), Ian Richardson (Ambassador
Toulon), Barbara Sukowa (Jeanne Gallimard)

Background

The play *M. Butterfly* by David Henry Hwang opened on Broadway in 1998
and ran for 777 performances. It was inspired by the real-life twenty-year
relationship between Bernard Boursicot, a clerk at the French embassy in
Beijing, and Shi Pei Pu, an opera singer who played female roles, and who
presented to the young Frenchman as a woman. Shi Pei Pu was an Uighur,
sold by his mother because the family was starving. Now a spy for the Chinese
government, Shi extracted secrets from Boursicot, convincing him along the
way that they had a son. After returning to his homeland, Boursicot and his
new lover Thierry arranged for Shi and the boy to come to Paris.

When the plot was exposed, Boursicot became the subject of ridicule in
France. In 1986, he and Shi were convicted of espionage and jailed. The
following year, for diplomatic reasons, Shi was pardoned and released.
Boursicot, hearing that Shi had always been a man, tried to commit suicide. He
failed and was released four months after Shi's pardon. This real-life tale, and
Madame Butterfly, inspired the play, which blends fact and fiction in its telling,
renaming the characters and changing certain details of their lives.

Peter Weir was approached to make a film version and turned it down.
Hearing that it was in development, David Cronenberg put himself forward. He
was a huge fan of the play.

As Gallimard, Jeremy Irons was a natural choice. Cronenberg cast John
Lone as Song Liling, and put his name on the poster, intentionally negating
any chance of a surprise. The director's reasoning was that he wanted the
best actor for the job, which was Lone. Barbara Sukowa, former protégée of
Fassbinder, took the role of Jeanne, Gallimard's deceived wife.

With a script by the playwright, filming took place in Toronto, Paris and
Hungary. One breathtaking moment was filmed at the Great Wall of China, the

vista falling away behind the characters. After Bertolucci's *The Last Emperor* (1987) opened China to Western filmmakers, shooting there must have seemed too good an opportunity to miss.

M. Butterfly made its debut at the Toronto International Film Festival on 9 September 1993, with other showings that month at the Sudbury film festival, Canada, and Thessaloniki in Greece. From there, it opened in the US in October, and the UK the following May.

The film did poorly at the box office and its reception was mixed. The *Globe and Mail* called it 'a beguiling masterpiece on the question of self-deception', and the *New York Times* said it was 'sometimes too flat and ambiguous for its own good'. Kim Newman, writing in *Empire*, lamented 'another step away from the singular vision Cronenberg once expressed even in his marginal works'.

Story

At the Beijing Opera, René Gallimard settles down to watch the performance: selections from *Madame Butterfly*, sung by diva Song Liling. It's 1964 and the Cold War is in play. René is an accountant at the French embassy, who appears to be sheltered somewhat from the culture of the country in which he works. After the performance, the Frenchman, struck by Song's voice, goes to meet her. He tells her that she has brought out the beauty in the story. But Song is having none of it. The story is appalling, presenting an orientalist view of Chinese women. This hadn't occurred to René. Song scolds his imperialism and insists the beauty of the opera is not in the words, but in the music. René is smitten.

He revisits the opera house, this time to hear Chinese music, and speaks again to Song, having lied to his wife about where he is going.

Contact with Song escalates; he visits her at home, inviting scandal. René kisses Song and she throws him out.

René isn't popular with his colleagues. At a party thrown by Frau Bauden, some of the embassy staff corner him and express their anger at his having turned down their expenses requests. He doesn't seem to understand how things are done, that a blind eye must be cast now and then.

Song has started to write to René, who does not reply. Something has grown in him, a confidence noted by the ambassador, who appoints René to the position of Vice Consul, and gives him the task of starting a new spy operation.

Emboldened, René goes to Song's house and they make love, though she remains clothed to protect her modesty, saying it's another Chinese custom that René doesn't understand. Song's maid watches balefully as this goes on.

Song and René progress their relationship, and even take a day trip to the Great Wall, against which they look insignificant.

At the embassy, the ambassador is writing a report on the situation in Vietnam. He asks René for his analysis. René says the Americans should remain strong, as the oriental will bow to a superior enemy.

The relationship continues with Song, who gets René to reveal valuable intelligence about the Americans. Song's handler, Chin, is the local Party official. He comes to visit and disdains her for having decadent movie star magazines in her room. Song counters that she is trying to be someone else.

René sleeps with Frau Bauden at one of her gatherings and tells her he's starting an *extra* extramarital affair with her. The experience appears to refresh him, as when he next meets Song, he asks to see her naked. Song counters that she's pregnant and must go to her parents' home village for her confinement. She will bring René back a son. Distracted by joy, René forgets his demand. Song meets Chin and asks him to provide her with a blond Chinese baby boy.

Sometime after Song has gone away, René passes a demonstration where opera costumes are being burned. The cultural revolution has turned its gaze on music.

Song brings her 'son' to meet his father. René proposes to her, but she can't stay, because the Red Guards have declared all artists to be criminals, and Song is being sent to a labour camp.

René has troubles of his own. The embassy sends him home to Paris for having wrongly assessed the situations in China and Vietnam. Before he goes, he tries to visit Song but finds that her house has been taken over by peasant workers. Song, visibly a man now in prison clothes, suffers in the camp. Over loudspeakers, a message booms out: hard labour will make them citizens of the future if they follow Mao's teachings.

Years go by and René's life has changed. It's 1968, and students are rioting in the streets. They chant slogans and hold up banners promoting communism. René attends the opera to hear *Madame Butterfly*, and he can't hold back his tears.

Then out of the blue, his butterfly returns. Song appears at his door, free at last to join him. René now works as a courier delivering diplomatic pouches. Song asks him to give her access to the secrets he carries. She tells him that she is being blackmailed, that their son is in danger if René doesn't cooperate. Blinded by paternal feelings, he does as she asks.

It isn't long before a government agent arrests him.

René is put on trial for espionage, and only now does he see the truth. Song, wearing a suit, is a man. Song tells the court how René gave him classified information to save their son. And did René know Song was a man? The question is left open. Song says that he invented 'oriental ways' to protect the deception.

In the police van taking them to prison, Song undresses to prove his masculinity, disgusted that René won't accept him now. René says that what he loved was the lie.

Months later, Song is extradited to China. As the plane goes through flight checks, a very different ritual is taking place elsewhere.

René sits in the prison square as his fellow inmates look on. He plays a tape of *Madame Butterfly* while wearing her clothes and wig, and holds up a small mirror to paint his face white and red. He spins the story of an oriental woman spurned by a man who was not worthy of her; but the woman is now René, and the man is Song. Bowing to the audience, René cuts his throat with the sharp edge of the mirror, then falls into death.

In a final image of separation, the steps detach from Song's aeroplane as it rolls off the apron towards the runway, preparing to fly away.

Comment

David Henry Hwang's screenplay for *M. Butterfly* necessarily loses the ambiguity that theatre allows for. On stage, a man playing a woman has been a tradition for centuries, just as in the opera Cho-Cho-San can be played by a white diva.

For technical reasons, the film cannot quite get away with this, the camera's gaze being so close and intense, but the clarity of John Lone's masculinity serves to make Gallimard's delusion all the more tragic. His arrogance and his refusal to see Song as other than female turns out to be his fatal flaw. All the while, Song chides him for his colonialist assumptions. In his professional life, Gallimard is revealed to have blinkered views, common at the time, that the 'oriental' will always bow to the might of the Americans, as he says to his boss. That assessment leads to his downfall.

Gallimard's flaws stand for the failure of imperialists to understand the *other*. In Vietnam, the United States' military-industrial-superiority complex helped its army to lose the war.

A similar transformation in Irish film director Neil Jordan's *The Crying Game* (1992) created word-of-mouth and turned the film into a hit. In response, as *M. Butterfly* was still in production, and he knew he couldn't compete with Jordan's twist, Cronenberg shot a scene for the start of his film to show clearly that Song was a man. This scene turned viewers off, so it was removed, and the ambiguity of Song's identity remained. However, there was no twist. By the end, it was clear that Song was always a man; Gallimard, blinded by infatuation and misled by Song, chose not to see it.

When asked if Gallimard is gay, Hwang says he is, because at some level he must have known that he was sleeping with a man. The playwright also doesn't consider Song Liling to be transgender, as the character himself doesn't.

Irons is suitably mooning as Gallimard, in a performance that anticipates his portrayals of other deluded men, in Louis Malle's *Damage* (1992) and Adrian Lyne's *Lolita* (1997). Lone plays Butterfly subtly as a character who barely conceals her disgust for Gallimard's prejudice.

Body horror enters the film towards the climax, with Gallimard's revulsion at seeing Song's male body. It also appears quite graphically in the Frenchman's prison suicide. Until that moment, *M. Butterfly* is one of Cronenberg's most subdued films.

Crash (1996)

Production: Alliance Communications Corporation, FineLine Features, The Movie
Network, Telefilm Canada, Recorded Picture Company
Produced by Chris Auty, David Cronenberg, Andras Hamori, Robert Lantos,
Stephane Reichel, Marilyn Stonehouse and Jeremy Thomas
Written by David Cronenberg from the novel by J. G. Ballard
Cinematographer: Peter Suschitzky
Music: Howard Shore
Directed by David Cronenberg
Filming dates: 27 September to 10 December 1995
Canada release: 4 October 1996
US release: 21 March 1997
UK release: 6 June 1997
Running time: 100 minutes
Budget: $9 million
Cast: Rosanna Arquette (Gabrielle), Holly Hunter (Helen Remington), Elias Koteas
(Vaughan), James Spader (James Ballard), Deborah Kara Unger (Catherine Ballard)

Background

J. G. Ballard put on an exhibition of crashed cars in April 1970 at a gallery
in London. Each display intended as a memorial to an individual meeting
between man and technology, the show made narrative art out of death and
injury. A naked model completed the sculpture, her presence a comment on
the frailty of the human body vs the brutality of the machine. Ballard's use of
sharp, metal wrecks juxtaposed with the yielding softness of skin in an erotic
conversation between the two, seemed outlandish enough to provoke violent
responses from some in the audience. Had this show been staged a generation
later, it could have won the Turner Prize.

Some of the ideas in 'Crashed Cars' were developed that same year in
Ballard's experimental book, *The Atrocity Exhibition*, which included a story
called *Crash!* The exclamation mark was dropped in the eventual novel
because it's implied. The whole book is about a particular kind of punctuation.
Crash (1973), which Ballard later called a 'psychopathic hymn', was not
intended as a cautionary tale.

In 1970, Ballard himself was the first to make a film of the material, with a
seventeen-minute docudrama based on his short story. Directed by Harvey
Cokeliss, this film is a meditative, fetishistic and violent argument for the 'man
in a car' as the defining image of the 20th century. *Crash!* features Gabrielle
Drake, who was about to appear in Gerry Anderson's *UFO*, and Ballard himself,
looking rather less like a television star.

The 'next one' would be made by David Cronenberg, whom Jeremy
Thomas, after *Naked Lunch*, considered the perfect director for *Crash*. As with
Burroughs, Ballard and Cronenberg were clearly in tune with each other's
aesthetic.

Ballard in the 1996 film, the audience viewpoint character, is played by James Spader. He applies his *sex, lies, and videotape* style to a character who is not impotent, in a drily erotic turn that he would refine in future films such as *Secretary* (2002). The story's key trickster is Vaughan, a catalyst for the madness. Elias Koteas plays him as the 'hoodlum scientist' of the book, with sleazy, demented conviction. Rosanna Arquette is Gabrielle, an out and proud disabled woman with whose leg wound Ballard has sex. Holly Hunter, who had been lobbying Cronenberg for a part in one of his movies, is stunning as the bereaved Helen Remington. As Ballard's self-possessed wife Catherine, Deborah Unger shows herself his equal in their open marriage, a fellow explorer of the unknown erotic.

Again, Howard Shore creates the soundtrack, an angular, metallic collision of electric guitars and other instruments, twisted like a car in a pile-up. Peter Suschitzky brings out the coldness of the story and the hollowness of the characters with a muted palette, autumnal and nocturnal, continuing his run of great-looking movies for Cronenberg.

Filming took place between September and December 1995 at various locations in and around Toronto. Some of the roads were closed off for the shoot, which was probably a wise move. The car showroom scene, one of the many hilarious moments in *Crash*, was shot at a real showroom on Dundas Street.

A quarter of a century later, the film has kept its power to shock. On release, that shock was sometimes expressed in the most reactionary terms. The *Daily Mail* ran a front-page headline: 'Ban This Car Crash Sex Film'. No greater accolade could a car crash sex film ask for.

At Cannes, *Crash* won a Special Jury Prize for originality, audacity and daring, an award which the jury invented for the film after president Francis Ford Coppola objected to giving it a mainstream prize. According to Cronenberg later, Coppola was himself the 'certain jury member' who 'did abstain passionately'. The prize has never been awarded since.

'Morally offended' Ted Turner, owner of the film's distributor Fine Line, tried to stop its release in the US but eventually *Crash* came out in the land of the freeway.

Some commentators were more upset than others. In England, the Conservative government's Heritage Secretary Virginia Bottomley, who hadn't seen *Crash*, called for Westminster council to ban the film, which they did. That didn't stop anyone from taking a short walk down Shaftesbury Avenue to see it in Camden. *Crash* remains banned in Westminster, a situation that resonates in the age of social media where the pre-emptive expression of outrage in expectation of offence, is how some people say hello.

Ireland passed the film with only one cut, but it was crucial erotic dialogue that illuminated character. *Film Ireland* bemoaned this excision, as anyone could buy the screenplay in a bookshop and read the full speech.

When it wasn't outraged, critical opinion was generally positive. Martin

Scorsese ranked *Crash* as the eighth-best film of the decade. Mark Kermode has called it a 'pretty much perfect film'.

In the 1990s, it wasn't likely that *Crash* would stay suppressed for too long. Today, it's unlikely that it would be made at all. Cronenberg suggested as much when asked in a 2020 interview marking the film's re-release in a beautiful new 4K print. We live in more conservative, censorious times, was his view.

As for J. G. Ballard's response? He thought the film was better than the book.

Story

James and Catherine Ballard stand on their balcony and reflect on the events of the day. Catherine had bent over the wing of a light aircraft in a hangar, pressing against the metal with her naked breast, as a man penetrated her from behind. Her husband James, a film director, had fucked a camera girl in a room on his film set. The Ballards discuss these couplings with mutual curiosity. Catherine had come, but James had not. She sympathises: 'Maybe the next one...' Now James fucks her from behind while below them passes the endless motion-sculpture of the motorway.

Ballard, out driving, has a crash, his car ploughing into another. The driver of the oncoming car is flung through the windscreen and is branded with an imprint of the car's insignia. As a stunned Ballard stares ahead, he spots a woman in the other car. She stares back at him. She's dazed and exposes her breast as she pulls on her seatbelt.

In hospital, Ballard recovers from his injuries. He's wearing a leg brace held with metal pins, as he gingerly walks down a corridor. The passenger whose car he hit, Helen Remington, regards him with disdain as she passes by. She is the widow of the driver killed in the accident.

Now a strange man approaches Ballard to photograph his injuries. He carries other photographs of wounds. He might be a doctor or a pornographer.

Catherine arrives at the hospital to find James in bed, in an otherwise empty ward. She has been to see the wreckage of his car. As she describes it, they masturbate each other, getting off on the damage.

James is now home from hospital and seems to have a newfound attraction to cars. From his balcony, he watches the motorway again. He thinks the volume of traffic has increased since he crashed.

Ballard drives to the pound to inspect his old vehicle. By coincidence or not, Helen Remington has come to see it too. She works at the airport; Ballard drives her there and they nearly have another accident. At the airport car park, they copulate intensely in the car, before Helen goes off to her job in immigration.

When Catherine and James next have sex, it seems turbocharged by his experience of Helen.

The situation escalates. Hoping to make sense of why their car crash has aroused them so, Helen invites James to an event put on by a man called Vaughan. This is a performance piece that reconstructs James Dean's death in the crash of *Little Bastard*, the young actor's Porsche race car. James recognises Vaughan as the man in the hospital who took such an interest in his leg brace.

An audience has gathered for the show, at an isolated woodland road. Vaughan and his drivers take to their cars as he narrates to the crowd via a microphone. The two cars crash into each other. Vaughan is visibly hurt. His co-driver is fine, but the driver of the other car is half-unconscious. Sirens announce the arrival of the authorities, the Department of Transport, whose agents break up the event, as Vaughan, Helen and Ballard escape in the provocateur's Lincoln convertible. Vaughan fingers Helen as he drives.

Vaughan takes them to the house where he and some of his followers live. One of the stunt drivers, Seagrave, is already back from the event, his wife taking care of his injuries. Another follower, Gabrielle, is a veteran of road accidents. She wears leathers, stockings and callipers to keep her broken body together. There is a vulva-shaped crash wound in the back of one of her legs, stitched up but not entirely closed. Her stockings eroticise the wound.

Gabrielle passes joints around. Many of the people here are already high. Vaughan's next project, recreating the death-crash of Jayne Mansfield, will be about more than just restaging a historical event. It will involve the 'reshaping of the human body' by technology. There's a political dimension to his endeavour. Meanwhile, his followers pore over photographs of crashes and watch test-dummy videos.

On the road, these acolytes haunt traffic accidents, rubbernecking the carnage and taking photographs for the collection. At one accident, Vaughan seems particularly messianic as he goes in to capture the moment with his pitiless camera.

James and Catherine, driving separate cars, stalk each other in the streets. They're hoping to crash together, to set off an erotic explosion. Vaughan is playing this game too. He creeps up in his Lincoln behind Catherine's car and follows her until she drives off the road.

As Catherine and James fuck in his car, Vaughan asks James how he would like to be sodomised.

Back in the airport garage, James fucks Helen as she describes some of the sex she has had in cars. She tells him of her desire to have Vaughan photograph them while they fuck.

Driving again around the airport roads, James and Vaughan discuss car crashes. Vaughan's Lincoln reminds the other man of the assassination of John F. Kennedy. Vaughan thinks of a car crash as a liberating, fertilising event rather than a destructive one. He picks up a prostitute at the airport and fucks her while Ballard drives the car and watches them in the rear-view mirror.

Leaving work at the film studio one day, James sees Catherine outside, and Vaughan in his car, being questioned by the police about the death of a pedestrian. James reckons that 'Vaughan isn't interested in pedestrians'. Still, his encounter with the police leaves Vaughan unsteady, so James drives him and Catherine onto the motorway.

They come to a crash, a multi-car pile-up, attended by the emergency services. In his ghoulish way, Vaughan jumps out and begins to take photographs of various victims and cars. Then he has an idea: he poses Catherine against the wreckage for further shots. No one stops him, as the ambulance and fire services have their hands full.

In one of the wrecks, Vaughan finds his stunt driver Seagrave wearing a wig and dressed as Jayne Mansfield. Taken aback that the stuntman performed the reconstruction without him, Vaughan decides to leave the scene. There's blood on his car.

In the carwash, the rollers block the interior of the Lincoln from view. Vaughan fucks Catherine roughly in the back seat while James watches them. Later he inspects the bruises Vaughan has left on his wife.

Further encounters follow. In the communal house, while watching videos of crashes, a clearly aroused Helen grabs the crotches of both James and Gabrielle.

At a car showroom, a flummoxed salesman helps Gabrielle into a shining new Merc, as her prosthetics and pins tear a hole in the seat. She's enjoying every minute.

Then at the airport, James has sex with Gabrielle, penetrating her vulva-mimicking leg wound.

Vaughan shows James the medical tattoo of a steering column on his chest. They have sex in a scrapyard, after which Vaughan crashes into a wrecked car in which James is sitting. The hoodlum scientist later rams Catherine's sports car.

On a road near the airport, James drives Catherine's car as Vaughan's Lincoln appears suddenly, playing with his prey, ramming it before swerving off an overpass and arcing down to hit a passenger coach on the motorway below. The wreckage is impressive. Vaughan dies in his last car accident.

The Lincoln has been taken to the car pound. Helen and Gabrielle fuck in its wreckage. Ballard arrives and claims the vehicle. He finds Catherine out driving and pursues her car, which he pushes off the road. Catherine's car tumbles down an embankment. Flung clear of the wreck, she lies on the grass, her skirt up over her hips. James rushes down to lie beside her. When Catherine tells him she's all right, he fucks her from behind. 'Maybe the next one', he says, as though they have both become Vaughan.

Comment

Crash, the book, is a reaction to the Boomer generation's sense of consumerist entitlement to sexual freedom, celebrating both the anarchy of boundaries being pushed, as well as satirising the jades, who needed ever more extreme stimuli to feel anything at all. They became automata as much as their cars were machines, which was one reason for their compatibility: vehicle and flesh conjoined in erotic collision.

The deadness of the characters in the novel masks a deep hunger for anything that will shake them out of it in a brief moment of impact. The car crash is a hit.

Whereas Ballard's book is written as a kind of pornographic manifesto for a new society, Cronenberg's film is a sly comment on the capitalist utopia that would follow the 'end of history'. We now know how that worked out.

Today, we can relate to both book and film. Our hyperstimulation creates its own kind of numbness, one that even an erotic car crash might not penetrate.

One crucial difference between the book and film is the aesthetic of the cars. Ballard, with his postwar admiration for American culture, 'a future that has fins in it', envied the glamour of those Pontiacs and Lincolns, those boudoirs on wheels, where you could imagine both the motorcade assassination in Dallas and an act of coitus taking place at the same time, in the same vehicle, in front of the same crowd of voyeurs and a live television audience of millions.

Ballard based the novel partly on events in his own life, as reported in his *roman à clef*, *The Kindness of Women*. Cronenberg updates the story to his present day, where cars are not so much *objets d'art* as Faraday cages with notions. This shift in aesthetic makes them less seductive, which somehow adds potency to the characters' desires in the film. Remove the fantasy of the classic American ride, and you eroticise the idea of the crash rather than the design of the car in which it takes place.

In this story, the one car that needs to be vintage is Vaughan's Lincoln. It is essential to both book and film, mostly because of the connotations mentioned above. Six Lincolns were used in production, including one which could have a camera mounted on it for POV shots, and one to be cut in two for ease of filming interiors.

The cars in the movie are all vintage now. So are the sex scenes, which act like the songs in a good musical: they reveal character and move the plot on. The sex in *Crash* holds the film together, and none of it is gratuitous.

In 2003, when Colin Powell spoke at the UN to justify the war his government and Britain's had already decided on, staff had to cover up a reproduction of Picasso's *Guernica* in the background so that its presence would not undermine the speech. Using the power of art to threaten the status quo, *Crash* also shows us who we really are. No wonder they tried to ban it.

eXistenZ (1999)

Production: Alliance Atlantis, Canadian Television Fund, The Canadian Film or
Video Production Tax Credit, Dimension Films, Existence Productions Limited, The
Harold Greenberg Fund/Le Fonds Harold Greenberg, The Movie Network, Natural
Nylon, Serendipity Point Films, Screenventures XXIV Productions Ltd. and Telefilm
Canada
Produced by Bradley Adams, Damon Bryant, David Cronenberg, Andras Hamori,
Robert Lantos, Michael MacDonald and Sandra Tucker
Cinematographer: Peter Suschitzky
Music by Howard Shore
Written and directed by David Cronenberg
Filming dates: 6 April to 8 July 1998
Canada release: 23 April 1999
US release: 23 April 1999
UK release: 30 April 1999
Running time: 97 minutes
Budget: $15 million
Cast: Willem Dafoe (Gas), Christopher Eccleston (Seminar Leader), Ian Holm (Kiri
Vinokur), Jude Law (Ted Pikul), Jennifer Jason Leigh (Allegra Geller), Don McKellar
(Yevgeni Nourish), Sarah Polley (Merle), Callum Keith Rennie (Carlaw), Robert A.
Silverman (D'Arcy Nader)

Background

Jennifer Jason Leigh completed filming on Stanley Kubrick's *Eyes Wide Shut*
(1999) and went on to her next job, *eXistenZ*. When Kubrick called her back
for retakes, she chose to stay with the Cronenberg film and Kubrick recast her
part. It was a sacrifice, perhaps, but *eXistenZ* seems to have been the more
enjoyable experience.

Casting difficulties also delayed production of *eXistenZ*, which had been
scheduled to go in 1997. Shooting began in April 1998 and lasted just over
three months, filming mostly at night at various locations in Toronto and
greater Ontario, including the Rockwood Conservation Area, doubling as the
countryside to which the protagonists flee.

Once the cast was in place, they proved a formidable line-up. Jennifer Jason
Leigh as Allegra Geller, gives a flinty, wry performance. *eXistenZ* is the first SF
outing for Christopher Eccleston, and another in Jude Law's run of excellent
genre films. The supporting players give it their all, particularly Ian Holm,
Willem Dafoe and Don McKellar.

The idea for the film arose from the director's interest in video games, as well
as his *Shift* magazine interview with Salman Rushdie, in which he discussed
the *fatwa*. The experience made Cronenberg wonder what if someone placed
a *fatwa* on a designer of virtual reality games. A simple premise, it made
for a mindbending story, Cronenberg's first entirely self-written piece since
Videodrome. MGM turned the project down but eventually several production

companies came on board, including Jude Law's Natural Nylon. Miramax took the film in the US, and Alliance distributed it in Canada.

There was competition, of course, 1999 being the year of both *The Phantom Menace* and *The Matrix*, but that man again, Roger Ebert, praised the film for being stranger and more organic than the Wachowskis' behemoth. At the box office, *eXistenZ* flopped. Maybe there was only so much unreality an audience could take.

Among its awards and nominations, the film won the Silver Bear at Berlin for the director's 'outstanding artistic contribution'. Nowadays, *eXistenZ* is often considered minor Cronenberg, but it was the first of his films that is simply great fun.

Story

It looks like an AA meeting, this gathering of ordinary people in a church hall, some sitting around in a half-circle on a stage, some in the audience. They are gamers, devotees, here to test *eXistenZ*, a new system from globally famous developer Allegra Geller, who is their special guest tonight.

In this world, biotech VR game pods have supplanted electronic gaming. Virtual reality has gone biological. Players have bio-ports surgically implanted into their spines; the pods connect to them via 'UmbyCords'. Game and player become one organism of flesh and mind. Two corporations compete for supremacy in the gaming field. They are Cortical Systematics and Antenna Research, for whom Geller works.

As she and her fans prepare to begin playing *eXistenZ*, the meeting is attacked. A 'Realist' terrorist, opposed to the fantasy of gaming, shoots Allegra in the shoulder with an organic pistol. The guards kill him and a man called Ted Pikul rescues Allegra, taking her outside to safety. She wonders if he's her protector and is less than impressed when he says he's a marketing trainee.

Allegra takes control of the situation, and they go on the run, driving away from the scene of the attack. On the road, she worries that her pod, which holds the only copy of *eXistenZ*, may have been corrupted by Realist agents. She needs Ted to play the game with her to find out if it has been damaged. But Ted, because of his phobia about being penetrated, has no bio-port. Allegra is taken aback and urges him to get one installed. Given what's at stake, Ted reluctantly agrees but asks where can he have it done, at a corner gas station?

Out in the countryside, they stop at a 'Corner Gas Station'. There, the only worker, a man called Gas, seems awestruck to meet Allegra. He installs a port in Ted's spine, inflicting excruciating pain on the young man, and the port turns out to be faulty.

Gas proves to be a hitman intent on picking up a bounty on Allegra's head, and Ted saves her by killing him. They run to a bolthole, a former ski lodge where Geller's old mentor Vinokur and his assistant live. He repairs her damaged game pod and replaces Ted's diseased port with a healthy one.

Entering *eXistenZ*, Allegra and Ted meet a man called Nader, who owns a video game store. He gives them two new micro-pods, which they activate, and they descend to a deeper level.

Instantly, they become workers in a factory, 'the trout farm', where game pods are produced. One of their colleagues, Nourish, tells them he is their contact, and they are all Realists. Allegra and Ted go to a Chinese restaurant where Nourish has recommended the special. This resembles a hideous mass of bones and flesh, like a half-eaten chicken that's been left for days. Ted messily consumes all the edible parts, then makes an organic pistol out of the bones that are left. It looks just like the 'gristle gun' that the intruder used to shoot Allegra in the church hall. On impulse, Ted aims the pistol at Allegra then he swerves to shoot and kill the waiter who brought them the special.

Returning to the video game store, they meet a man called Carlaw, who tells them that Nourish is a double agent and that the waiter Ted killed was their contact.

After lunch, they're back in the factory where Allegra finds a diseased pod which she attaches to her bio-port. She intends to undermine the factory but soon becomes sick from the disease in the pod. Seeing her distress, Ted cuts her UmbyCord. Allegra begins to bleed a grey ooze. Now Nourish comes back, wielding a flamethrower. He uses it to destroy the infected game pod, but the pod bursts open and projects spores everywhere.

Waking up at the ski lodge, Ted and Allegra find that her game pod is now also infected. Did Vinokur deliberately sabotage Ted's bio-port to infect *eXistenZ*? It seems likely. Allegra inserts a disinfectant into Ted's port and –

Carlaw reappears. He's now a resistance fighter on the side of the Realists. He takes Allegra and Ted from the ski lodge and assures them that they are about to witness the end of *eXistenZ*.

On the hill outside, a firefight rages. Vinokur shoots Carlaw in the back before telling Allegra that he copied her game while repairing her pod and that he works for Cortical Systematics. Allegra retaliates by shooting Vinokur. Then Ted declares himself to be a Realist agent sent to assassinate 'the demoness Allegra Geller'. However, Allegra has known this since the Chinese restaurant, and she remotely explodes Ted's bioport. His body blows up. The game is over.

Instantly, Allegra and Ted find themselves back in the church hall at the focus group. They recognise some of the gamers in real life, as characters they saw in the game. *Nourish* is here, and it seems that he is the true designer. Allegra only played that role inside the game, which Nourish calls *transCendenZ*. He confides in his assistant Merle that he's worried about the anti-gamer strain in the plot, which might have been introduced by one of the players.

Ted and Allegra, or the people who played them, now come up to Nourish and condemn him as an anti-Realist. They shoot him and and then they go to leave the church hall. At the door, they meet the man who played the waiter in the Chinese restaurant. They raise their guns to shoot him, but he begs mercy. Then he asks if they are still in the game. By their expressions, it seems that neither Ted Pikul nor Allegra Geller can say for sure.

Comment

From *Videodrome* to video games. With *eXistenZ*, his first wholly self-written film in sixteen years, David Cronenberg returned to the subject of alternative realities. Back then, other films that played with this idea included Douglas Trumbull's *Brainstorm* (1983) and Ken Russell's *Altered States* (1980), each very different.

By the time *eXistenZ* came to be made, 1990s cinema was awash with a new wave of virtuality, from *The Lawnmower Man* (1992) to the Joe-90 antics of *Johnny Mnemonic*, to the damaged souls of Kathryn Bigelow's *Strange Days* (both 1995). If Cronenberg's ideas seemed less fresh now, it was partly because his influence had spread. The works of William Gibson, Burroughs, Philip K. Dick and other fabulists, had also caught on with the moviegoing public. Cronenberg differentiated his film by setting it in the countryside, making it a non-urban political road movie littered with wrecked heads. Dick's novel *The Three Stigmata of Palmer Eldritch* appears to have influenced the concept of matryoshka realities in *eXistenZ*, which also reminds the viewer of Christopher Priest's literary landscape, Wessex. Hired to pen the film's novelisation, the English New Wave giant used his pseudonym, John Luther Novak. He told an interviewer later that he didn't think the VR in *eXistenZ* was very original. That may be, but depictions of technology in film usually lag behind those in literature. Putting *realistic* VR on screen in 1999 was impractical unless you had the resources of the Wachowskis. Then again, if the virtuality had to be so good that it was indistinguishable from the real world, why not use the real world and say it's a perfect recreation? That's what Cronenberg did, saving the film from looking dated by the limits of its CGI. Another adaptation came out, the graphic novel credited to illustrator Sean Scoffield and Cronenberg himself, but the true medium of *eXistenZ* is the film. Its dream-transition schema is decipherable if you know where to look for the clues, such as the changes in characters' hairstyles.

As a viewer, it was good to play in this world again, which feels like it belongs with *Videodrome* and its analogue aesthetic. The future here is retrofitted, the rural-virtual setting making it seem to exist outside of time. The political factions remind us of the totalitarian countercultures in *Scanners* and *Videodrome*. As for its resonance today, when *eXistenZ* came out, Google, with its mission statement, 'Don't Be Evil', was not eight months old. Facebook, Twitter, and so on, did not exist. *eXistenZ* now looks like a world in which such corporations or their usurpers, have taken power from subservient nation-states and compliant populations. It couldn't happen here.

With this, his last SF film, either David Cronenberg was putting away his toys, or he was picking them up again after a run of adaptations. Flesh penetrated by tech, rebels shouting unlikely slogans, organic weaponry, heightened dialogue, characters with funny names: they were all present and correct. Calling one of your characters Pikul and another Vinokur surely counts as a knowing joke. It's all fun and games until someone loses a third eye. And the ending is a stunner.

Spider (2002)

Production: Artists Independent Network, The Canadian Film or Video Production
Tax Credit, A Catherine Bailey/Artists Independent Network/Grosvenor Park
Production, Capitol Films, Davis Films, Odeon Films, Spider Productions Limited/
Spider Films Limited and Telefilm Canada
Produced by Catherine Bailey, Jane Barclay, David Cronenberg, Charles Finch,
Martin Katz, Hannah Leader, Sharon Harel and Luc Roeg
Written by Patrick McGrath from his novel
Cinematographer: Peter Suschitzky
Music by Howard Shore
Directed by David Cronenberg
Cast: Gabriel Byrne (Bill Cleg), Ralph Fiennes (Dennis 'Spider' Cleg), Bradley Hall
(Dennis as a boy), Lynn Redgrave (Mrs Wilkinson), Miranda Richardson (Yvonne,
Mrs Cleg), John Neville (Terrence)
Filming dates:
Canada release: 9 September 2002 (TIFF)
US release: 1 September 2002 (Telluride Film Festival), 23 February (limited)
UK release: 21 July 2002 (Cambridge Film Festival), 3 January 2003 (general)
Running time: 98 minutes
Budget: $10 million

Background

Patrick McGrath, the author of the novel *Spider*, adapted it as a screenplay and
sent it to David Cronenberg on spec. He included a note that Ralph Fiennes
had shown interest, but this was not what got the director's attention as much
as the script itself. After four pages, Cronenberg decided he wanted to make
this film.

The budget would be two-thirds that of *eXistenZ*, which had lost money. To
help with the financing, Cronenberg deferred his own salary. His lead actors,
Fiennes and Miranda Richardson did the same, as did the film's producers.
It was likely not a decision any of them relished financially, but artistically it
would prove very much worth it.

The film had scientific rigour on its side. Patrick McGrath, born in London,
had grown up near Broadmoor Hospital, where his father worked. He began
his career after college, working in Penetang Mental Health Centre in Ontario.
Spider, as with much of his fiction, was informed by these experiences. Dennis
Cleg's condition is a real one: the Capgras delusion, in which the sufferer
believes that someone close to them, a family member, friend or even pet,
has been replaced by an impostor who is identical. This idea finds its greatest
expression in popular cinema in the *Invasion of the Body Snatchers* films, to
rather different ends from how it is used here. The delusion is most commonly
found in people with paranoid schizophrenia. In other words, there's nothing
extraordinary about the horror in *Spider*. It is very real.

Cronenberg and McGrath agreed that although Spider himself narrates the novel, a voice-over would diminish the power of the character in the film. The writer revised his script accordingly. Instead, the director asked Fiennes to devise a handwriting style for Spider's diary, involving glyphs that the viewer couldn't decipher.

Spider was shot over eight weeks in 2001 in Canada and England with some filming in Toronto. Locations included Eton college; St Pancras Station, London; and Haggerston Gasworks in Bethnal Green, the East End location where Spider's halfway house and childhood stomping ground are set.

It's clear that Samuel Beckett's work is an inspiration on McGrath's novel. So it is with the film. David Cronenberg pinned photos of the great Irish playwright around the set. Ralph Fiennes's severe haircut is modelled on Beckett's own style.

Spider premiered on 21 May 2002 at Cannes and a month later to the day in the UK, at the Cambridge Film Festival. It rolled out in various territories over the next two years, from general release in Ireland and the UK on 3 January 2003, to Venezuela on 11 March 2005. It was a smash hit with critics. Peter Bradshaw in the *Guardian* called it 'an intensely controlled, beautifully designed and fascinatingly acted account of Patrick McGrath's original novel'. *Cahiers du Cinéma* named it as one of their top ten films of 2002.

At the box office, it did badly. Yet *Spider* remains one of the finest films in the careers of all involved, a credit to their tenacity and selflessness in getting it made.

Story

Thatcher's England in the 1980s, looking like the 1950s. An emotionally wounded man in a coat that, like himself, has seen better days, gets off a train after all the other passengers have gone. He is Dennis Cleg, known as Spider, carrying a battered suitcase. A paranoid schizophrenic, Spider mumbles his speech and walks with a defensive hunch in his gait, always prepared to retract like a hedgehog. His nails are long and dirty, his fingers stained with nicotine.

He has a piece of paper with an address on it: the halfway house to which he is being released. When he finds the place, it seems to fit his personality. A grim East London street that belongs to the past, some of the windows boarded up, a pervasive grey atmosphere. It's the area in which he grew up. The scene of the crime.

Across the road from the house, a gasometer tower looms like a cage, or a metal web reminding him of his past and perhaps of his future. The dark, threatening sounds that leak out from the tank of the gasometer, reflect the eggshell fragility of his mind.

The landlady, Mrs Wilkinson, ushers Spider into the house and he begins his transition to freedom. She runs the house with an iron will; her expression drained of any warmth, her demeanour curt. Perhaps this is her idea of professional distance. She shows Spider to his room. There, he starts to work on his notebook, in which he writes using marks and glyphs that don't resemble the English he speaks. Meaningful to him alone, these marks protect his thoughts from discovery by others. When he's not working on the notebook, he hides it under a threadbare rug in his room. Sometimes he pulls it out and scrawls anxiously in it as if to expel a troubling thought.

The guests in the house include Terrence, a psychotic but gentle old man who sounds like an actor born to the 19th-century stage. He's obsessed with scorpions, which seems to reflect Dennis's fascination with spider webs. One of the others, Freddy, is a middle-aged man who thinks Sophia Loren is in love with him.

Mrs Wilkinson gives Dennis a bath, the water spurting out rustily. He curls up in the tub, unable to return to any other kind of womb.

Dennis moves through this new world on a journey to the old. He wanders these streets with their blocked-up windows, the gas tower offering reproach as he descends in his mind to formative incidents from his youth. Spider is back in his neighbourhood, back in his childhood. He remembers his 13-year-old self, a morose boy whose eyes betray his fear. Young Dennis is fixated on spiders' webs, and objects that resemble them. The gas tower, the strings he keeps in his pocket – their lines, angles and patterns all feed into his obsession. He is disturbed when he can't solve a jigsaw. His mother names him Spider and tells him a story about female arachnids laying egg sacs then going off to die. The idea of a mother's sacrifice follows him for life.

Dennis watches his young self, who makes patterns with string as his mother prepares dinner. The boy builds elaborate cobwebs in his bedroom, using the string he has collected.

Old Spider also looks back on his parents' marriage. His father, Bill, works as a plumber. He spends most evenings in the pub, where he meets women for sex. When Spider's mother sends him to the pub to bring his father back, the boy catches sight of three prostitutes, one of whom flashes a breast at him as she and her friends cackle. The boy is further confused by seeing his mother posing before a mirror, wearing a slip. He sees his father getting hand-relief from one of the prostitutes, Yvonne, under a bridge. Meanwhile, Spider's mother, deserted in the evenings, declines into a resentful shadow of herself.

In the present day, Dennis starts to confuse his memories of his mother with Mrs Wilkinson.

A flashback changes everything. Spider sees his father having sex with Yvonne in the shed in his allotment. When Mrs Cleg finds them, Bill gets angry and kills her with a spade then buries his wife in the allotment, all the while egged on by his scarlet woman.

Bill brings Yvonne home, telling the boy that she is his mother, and Spider can't accept it. He knows the truth. One night he knocks Yvonne unconscious and gasses her to death in the oven. Bill comes in to find that his son has killed his loving wife.

The return of this memory so disturbs the adult Spider that he takes scissors to Mrs Wilkinson's room. He now confuses her with both Yvonne and his mother. But the landlady wakes up in bed and catches him with the scissors. Startled, she cries out, 'What have you done, Mr Cleg?' Her challenge shocks him into backing away.

A car comes to take him back to the asylum. Spider looks out as it drives away. Perhaps he will now put an end to his tormented life, lost in a web of his own weaving.

Comment

This beautiful, austere and disturbing film is not a horror. *Spider* is instead David Cronenberg's saddest movie, a granular portrait of schizophrenia in a man with a wounded mind, and a reminder that our idea of reality is always provisional.

The book is as much about character and mood as plot, but the articulation of Spider's thoughts in the novel is not possible in a film without a voice-over. If we are to believe in Spider's hell, it will not do for us to hear his thoughts. The glyphs written in Spider's diary make no literal sense but carry the weight of all that obscured meaning, illustrating how protective he must be of his privacy.

The film layers plot elements in a dreamlike way, adding to the story's poignancy. There is a twist in the tale, but it's no *Sixth Sense*. Nor is it done for shock value. The ending is inevitable and disturbing, making a powerful point on how lost people sometimes stay lost. Spider is both perpetrator and victim, newly revealed to himself, horrified at what he sees. He is also his own judge and perhaps executioner. At the end, although Spider lives, it might not be for long. Like the film poster says, the only thing worse than losing your mind is finding it again.

Spider is one of Cronenberg's most resonant films, not easily forgotten. The acting is top-notch. Fiennes is at his committed best, putting in a precisely calibrated, detailed performance of true emotional depth, crafted to perfection. Miranda Richardson is the film's secret weapon as Yvonne and Mrs Cleg. Without those characters working, the film would fall apart, and Richardson makes them both distinctive and believable. And what is it with David Cronenberg and doubles in his films? Gabriel Byrne is his usual fine self as the father, a variation on a role he played in Richard E. Grant's *Wah Wah*, though here the father is maligned by his child's unreliable memory. Lynn Redgrave and John Neville give sterling support as the hatchety landlady and the demented old man, respectively.

Neville as Terrence appears to show what Dennis might eventually evolve into. He also has the film's funniest lines, one of which sums things up quite neatly. 'Clothes maketh the man, and the less there is of the man, the more the need of the clothes.'

Right: *From the Drain* (1967). Two men and a parasite in a bath. (*Arrow Video*)

Left: *Stereo* (1969). The Toronto University campus stands in for the future of architecture. (*Arrow Video*)

Right: *Crimes of the Future* (1970). Lobby card.

emergent films presents CRIMES of the FUTURE a film by david cronenberg
in eastmancolor

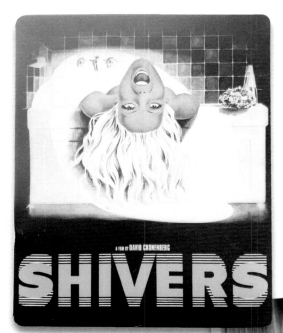

Left: *Shivers* (1975). Steelbook with artwork based on the poster. (*Arrow Video*)

Above & Left: The many names, and creative advertising presentations, of *Shivers*. (Various)

Right: *Rabid* (1977). Quad poster showing the full horror of the rage.

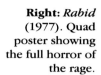

Left: *Fast Company* (1979). French-language poster that gives a pretty good indication of the film's tone.

Below: Lonnie (William Smith) and Adamson (John Saxon) try to iron out a few disagreements. (*Blue Underground*)

Left: *The Brood* (1979). What a rage monster looks like in utero, probably…

Below: How to get ahead in telepathy. Revok (Michael Ironside), about to blow the mind of another scanner (Louis Del Grande). (*Arrow: VTV Belgium*)

Left: A poster for *Scanners* (1981).

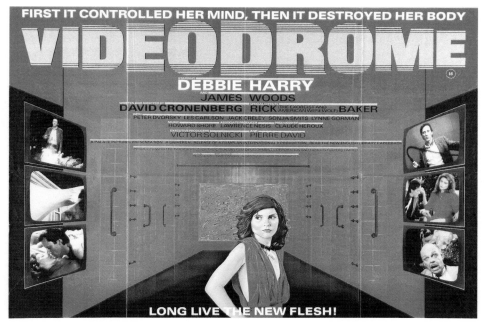

Above: *Videodrome* (1983). This UK poster promoted Debbie Harry as the star of *Videodrome*.

Below: Is that a gun fusing with your hand or are you just pleased to see me? The new flesh in action. (*Arrow Video*)

Above: Quad poster for *The Dead Zone* (1983). Stark and powerful and *very* Stephen King.

Below: Johnny and Sarah get together one last time. (*Prism Leisure*)

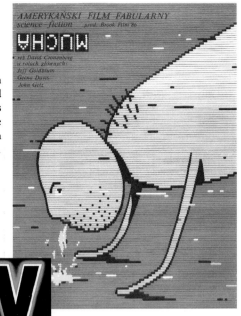

Right: *The Fly* (1986). Polish film posters are renowned for startling imagery. This one thinks outside the telepod to encapsulate fusion perfectly…

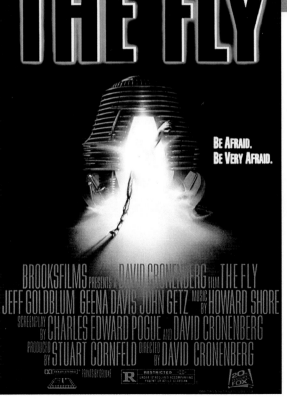

Left: …and the original, iconic, American poster.

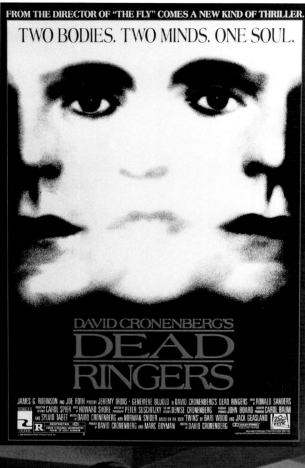

Left: A poster for *Dead Ringers*.

Below: The Mantle twins (Jeremy Irons) in *Dead Ringers* (1988). (*ITV Global Entertainment*)

Right: Your invitation to dine. *Naked Lunch* poster, 1991.

Below: What's a nice Mugwump like you doing in a place like this? (*Optimum Releasing*)

Left: *M. Butterfly* poster (1993).

Below: Song (John Lone) and René (Jeremy Irons) enjoy a day out by the wall. (*Widemedia*)

Right: Poster for *Crash* (1996) featuring James Spader and Holly Hunter.

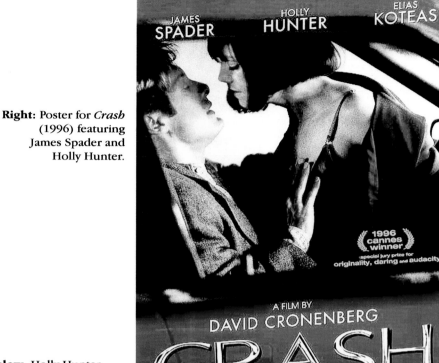

Below: Holly Hunter as Helen Remington in *Crash* (1996). (*Turbine Media*)

Left: *eXistenZ* Blu-ray (2018, limited edition cover, based on the original poster.) (*101 Films Black Label*)

Below: Allegra Geller (Jennifer Jason Leigh) and friend. (*101 Films Black Label*)

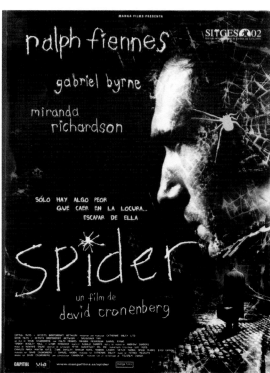

Right: Sitges film festival poster for *Spider* (2002).

Below: *A History of Violence* (2005) film poster.

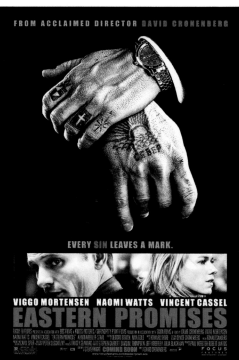

Left: Tattoos maketh the man. *Eastern Promises* poster (2007).

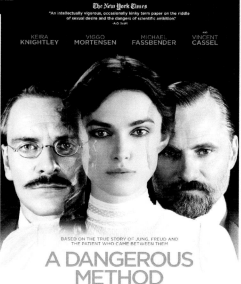

Right: *A Dangerous Method* film poster (2011).

Above: French Language poster for *Cosmopolis* (2012).

Below: Eric (Robert Pattinson) and Jane (Emily Hampshire) have a meeting. Proctologist just out of shot. (*Entertainment One*)

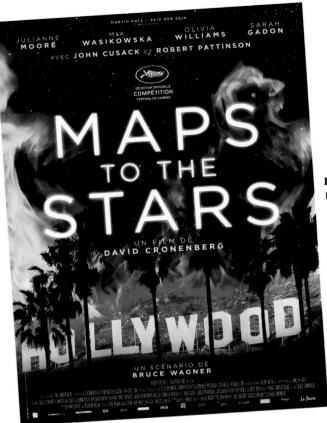

Left: *Maps to the Stars* film poster (2014).

Below: Agatha's back to burn this town. (*Entertainment One*)

A History of Violence (2005)

Production: BenderSpink, Media II Filmproduktion München GmbHH & Co. KG0, New Line Productions, Inc.
Produced by Kent Alterman, Josh Braun, Chris Bender, Cale Boyter, Toby Emmerich, Justis Greene, Roger E. Kass, J.C. Spink, Jake Weiner
Written by Josh Olson from the graphic novel by John Wagner and Vince Locke
Cinematographer: Peter Suschitzky
Music: Howard Shore
Directed by David Cronenberg
Filming dates: 2 August to 14 November 2004
Canada release: 10 September 2005 (TIFF)
US release: 23 September 2005 (limited); 30 September 2005 (wide)
UK release: 30 September 2005
Running time 96 minutes
Budget: $32 million
Cast: Maria Bello (Edie Stall), Ed Harris (Carl Fogarty), Ashton Holmes (Jack Stall), William Hurt (Richie Cusack), Peter MacNeill (Sheriff Sam Carney), Stephen McHattie (Leland), Viggo Mortensen (Tom Stall, Joey Cusack)

Background

Because *eXistenZ* and *Spider* had lost money and he needed a payday, David Cronenberg finally arrived at his 'selling out' film. *A History of Violence*, based on the 1997 graphic novel by John Wagner and Vincent Locke, was it. Creator of Judge Dredd in Britain's punk-SF comic, *2000 AD*, Wagner was known for hard-hitting stories of futurecrime and ultraviolence, laced with gallows humour.

Cronenberg and casting director Deirdre Bowen assembled a powerful company of actors. Viggo Mortensen plays Tom Stall, our conflicted protagonist. Maria Bello is Edie, Tom's wife. Ed Harris cameos as a mobster who calls on Tom to return home. William Hurt, playing the brother of Mortensen's character, gives a truthful, complex performance as a brutal man surrounded by the trappings of power and privilege. Not someone you want to cross, he waits at the end of the film, a sharp-suited nemesis.

A History of Violence was shot between 2 August and 14 November 2004, mainly in Millbrook, Ontario, a town that shares its name with the fictional setting of the story, Millbrook, Indiana. A popular filming location, Millbrook ON looks just like Main Street, USA, given a little set dressing, and swapping out the flags. Cronenberg chose it to evoke the kind of perfect American town you might find in *The Twilight Zone*. He considered Millbrook as 'maybe too perfect, and that's part of the playing with the mythology of Americana, the America that America itself wants to believe'. The diner on King Street is 'very Edward Hopper-ish', the director says in the DVD commentary. Its frontage was used for scenes set outside Tom's restaurant. Scenes set inside were shot at the Toronto Film Studios. Eaton Hall, a suitably dark mansion in King City, Ontario, stands in for the house in Philadelphia, the 'labyrinth' Tom enters at the end to face his reckoning and resolve his classic antihero's journey.

Production finished in December and the film was released at Cannes on 16 May 2005. It opened in Canada on 10 September to near universal acclaim and a host of awards. William Hurt and writer Josh Olson received Oscar nominations.

Starting as a commercial proposition whose style appeared uncharacteristically straight, *A History of Violence* turned out as one of the director's finest films. Some critics considered it a return to form, but it's hard to see that he had lost any, his previous film being so remarkable. They meant that this was his commercial revival, but it is still very much a Cronenberg picture. Mark Kermode named *A History of Violence* the best film of 2005. Viggo Mortensen later called it 'a perfect film noir'.

Story
Tom Stall is a quiet, unassuming man who owns a diner in Millbrook, Indiana. His wife, Edie, is a lawyer. His children, Jack and Sarah, complete this idyllic setup. No one could appear more normal and well-adjusted than Tom Stall, until one night his world is turned upside-down.

Two armed men burst into his diner and try to rob it. When it looks like one of the robbers is going to assault a waitress, Tom reacts suddenly with modulated violence, killing the men expertly and efficiently.

The story makes the news, turning Tom into a local hero. His family and the townsfolk admire him and no one asks where he got such skills. Tom's celebrity soon attracts unwanted attention as the story reaches beyond Millbrook. A scarred gangster called Carl Fogarty turns up at the diner along with his henchmen. He's here to see Tom, who Carl accuses of being a gangster, Joe Cusack from Philadelphia. Tom denies Carl's allegations but the scarred man isn't going anywhere. He sticks around in Millbrook and begins to stalk Tom's wife and children while Tom is at work.

Carl's harassment, and Tom's sudden notoriety, put a strain on the family. Edie doesn't understand what the man could possibly want with her husband.

Jack, their teenage son, has a fight at school when he stands up to a bully, using force against his tormentor and getting in trouble as a result. At home, Jack and Tom fall out over this incident. Jack wants to know why self-defence is good enough for his father but not for him. Jack runs away from home and Fogarty catches him.

Now holding Jack hostage, Fogarty and his men go up to the house and demand that Cusack/Tom return with them to Philadelphia. Cusack has unfinished business there.

Tom agrees to go with them and the gangsters release Jack, but Tom approaches the men too slowly, so they try to grab him. He kills two of them, then Fogarty shoots Tom to save himself. A wounded Tom lies on the ground and as Fogarty prepares to finish him off, Tom admits the truth. He is Joe Cusack.

Before Carl Fogarty can kill his father, Jack shoots and kills the gangster.

Tom is brought to hospital, where Edie challenges him. She has seen who he really is, and Tom again admits his identity. He has killed people, sometimes for pay, sometimes because he enjoyed it, but he insists that he left the gang life behind in Philadelphia, and the man Edie married is who he is now.

After Tom is released from hospital, the sheriff, Sam, comes to talk to the couple at home. Sam is mystified by the events surrounding Tom. It seems to him that the gangsters are going to a lot of trouble, so they must be sure they've got the right man. Edie steps in, preventing Tom's confession. She says Tom is who he claims to be. He's Tom Stall, her husband. Edie begins to cry, and Sam, more confused than before, leaves the house.

After Sam has gone, Edie and Tom begin to fight. Slaps at first, then it gets more violent as Tom chases Edie and they have hard sex on the sharp stairs.

In the days that follow, Edie and Jack keep their distance from Tom. Edie isn't sure what to make of his revelations, and their relationship grows tense and cold.

Everything changes again when Tom gets a call from Philadelphia. It's his brother Richie Cusack, who wants 'Joe' to come home, or he will go to Millbrook to find him. Joe agrees to Richie's demand, and he travels to the city of brotherly love.

Richie lives in opulence but his life is empty. After Joe bailed out, having offended several gangsters, they took it out on Richie, stifling his progress in the gang's hierarchy and penalising him financially. Joe offers the hand of friendship, but for Richie it's too late. He calls for his men to kill Joe. With speed and skill, Joe kills them instead then escapes into the house. Richie and his last man standing search for Joe, whose stealth gives him the advantage. He kills both men then leaves his old life in Philadelphia behind for a second time.

When the man returns home, it is unclear whether he is Tom or Joe. His wife and children wait at the dinner table. He enters and sits down. His family stare over at him and he gazes back at them.

Comment

A History of Violence was the last major Hollywood thriller released on VHS, appearing on the format in 2006. Based on its storyline, the film had the potential to become a straight-to-video exploitation picture, but David Cronenberg and his collaborators made a deeper film, one that uses pulp tropes to meditate on the appalling effects of violence on a life, a family, and a community. The title can be understood in many ways apart from the obvious. For a story set in a country where unpredictable violence is a daily threat, the title calls attention to the film as a critique of America seen through the eyes of a Canadian. *Batman Begins*, a blockbuster take on vigilantism, was released the same year, but *A History of Violence* was not eclipsed. It is interested in exploring violence as a human experience. There are no superheroes here although there is myth, the Stall family's tragedy playing out like a gangster western. The film is one of the best made from a comic.

For much of his career, Cronenberg had been infusing genre pieces with penetrating psychological insight, and so it is here. A study of secrets and their consequences, the film also investigates PTSD. Who returns from Philadelphia at the end and what is he capable of? Like a shell-shocked war veteran, is Tom now too damaged for his marriage to survive without others having to make unbearable compromises? It is the Michael Corleone question. What blind eye must Edie turn if she is to tell herself that everything is now all right?

A History of Violence is also ghost story, the restless spirit needing redress or recognition. Tom's ghost is himself. He must accept Joe before both can be free. At the end, it's unclear whether he has done this. It is not always possible to pay a debt by murdering those to whom it is owed, and there is still a deficit in Tom's account.

The incident at the diner sets the tone for what follows, leaving a powder of dread in the air and introducing a tension that tautens until something must give. The robbery serves a 'payment due' notice on Tom's Faustian pact with his other identity.

Viggo Mortensen puts in a bravura, award-winning performance, his best to date. Calm on the surface and seething beneath, his character's dynamic is the same as that of the Hulk or Superman, an ordinary man with a secret identity. Except Tom cannot save anyone, least of all himself. Violence itself is Tom's home ground, whatever name he goes by. Mortensen is right in his assessment of the film. A mature exploration of serious themes, this is a compelling modern noir, a fascinating character study, and a warning to us all.

Eastern Promises (2007)

Production: Kudos Pictures, Serendipity Point Films, Telefilm Canada, Corus
Entertainment, BBC Films, Scion Films, Astral Media
Distribution: Focus Features, Alliance Atlantis
Produced by Paul Webster, Robert Lantos
Written by Steven Knight (as Steve Knight)
Cinematographer: Peter Suschitzky
Music: Howard Shore
Directed by David Cronenberg
Filming dates: 19 November 2006 to 16 February 2007
Canada release: 8 September 2007 (TIFF)
US release: 14 September 2007 (limited), 21 September 2007 (wide)
UK release: 17 October 2007 (London Film Festival), 26 October 2007 (general)
Running time: 100 minutes
Budget: $50 million
Cast: Vincent Cassel (Kirill), Sinéad Cusack (Helen), Viggo Mortensen (Nikolai),
Armin Mueller-Stahl (Semyon), Naomi Watts (Anna)

Background

For *Eastern Promises*, his first film shot entirely outside Canada, David
Cronenberg directs a taut script by Steven Knight. The writer, known at that
time for *Dirty Pretty Things*, would later be acclaimed for writing and directing
the superlative *Locke* (2013).

This movie marks a break in Cronenberg's run of literary adaptations but
is impeccably literate, a brutal and tense exploration of the violence men
do. A London film through and through, *Eastern Promises* began shooting
in November 2006. Locations included Broadway Market in Hackney for the
scenes in Azim's Hair Salon; Brompton cemetery; and the Farmiloe Building
for Semyon's Trans-Siberian restaurant. Anna's hospital, the Trafalgar, was
shot in the abandoned Middlesex Hospital, shortly before its demolition in
2007. The Post Office tower, once the pinnacle of modernity, stood sentinel in
the background. The film's most notorious scene, the knife fight in the steam
room, was shot on a set modelled on the Ironmonger Row baths.

Viggo Mortensen plays Nikolai, a man with a secret, who is dedicated to his
duty. Naomi Watts is Anna, a decent, determined midwife, and the moral heart
of the film. Armin Mueller-Stahl is Seymon, on the surface a friendly patriarch
but underneath, a hollowed-out devil. Vincent Cassell plays Kirill, the no-good
wastrel with a mean streak. Rounding out the cast, Anna's parents are finely
drawn by Sinead Cusack and film director Jerzy Skolimowski.

Researching his role, Viggo Mortensen consulted an expert on the Russian
mafia and the use of tattoos in their culture. After he inadvertently terrified the
diners in a Russian restaurant with his fake skin-art, from then on, Mortensen
had the tattoos washed off when he left the set. This experience underlined
just how potent these symbols are.

To intensify the action, Cronenberg gave his gangsters knives rather than guns, specifically carpet knives that in the wrong hands can tear flesh from bone. The idea was that gangsters would carry these 'innocent tools' to give them plausible deniability if stopped by police.

Eastern Promises was released on 8 September 2007 at the Toronto International Film Festival, where it won the Audience Prize for Best Film. It did well in the US and Canada in limited release and continued to win awards. Most critics applauded the film as one of the director's best, including J. Hoberman at the *Village Voice*, who praised its 'brooding power' and called it 'a masterful mood piece'. The film left a door open for a sequel but the screenplay for that, after budget issues derailed the project, has now been reworked for an unrelated film. Perhaps that's just as well. The question left hanging at the end of *Eastern Promises* contains its own answer.

Story

In a London barbershop, a Chechen man waits for his haircut. A young assassin comes in and slits the man's throat with a straight razor. Blood pools on the floor. The man is dead. The killer flees the scene.

Tatiana, a 14-year-old girl, turns up at a pharmacy. She's distressed, haemorrhaging, collapsing.

Anna Khitrova, of Russian heritage, is a midwife on shift at Trafalgar hospital when Tatiana is rushed in. She helps deliver the baby, but its mother dies. Anna finds a diary on Tatiana's body and takes it away, hoping it will give her a clue about the dead girl. She also finds a business card for a restaurant, the Trans-Siberian. The diary is written in Russian, but Anna cannot translate it. Her priority is to find a home for Tatiana's daughter, and her only lead is that card.

She goes to the restaurant and meets its owner, Semyon, an affable old man, who offers to help her. Secretly he is a *vor*, the London head of a Russian mafia gang.

Anna tells her mother and uncle about Tatiana, the baby, and her own desire to help the child. She also mentions Semyon. Although her mother Helen is sympathetic, her uncle Stepan warns her to take care, as she doesn't know who she's dealing with: Tatiana was a prostitute. He agrees to translate the diary.

What he discovers is quite horrifying. Tatiana was trafficked. Kirill, Semyon's son, had attempted to rape her but failed. Semyon raped her instead. Then they had her addicted to heroin and put into prostitution. Tatiana, dead at fourteen, was a victim of the men whom Anna has asked for help. Now that she knows Semyon is the baby's father, her own family might be in danger.

She meets Nikolai, who works as a driver for Semyon. He is also a *cleaner*, who destroys evidence, including murdered bodies, which he dumps in the Thames. Seemingly taking pity on the plight of the child, Nikolai brokers a deal between Semyon and Anna. The gangster will give her the location of Tatiana's family if Anna will hand over the incriminating diary. Anna agrees and hands the diary to Nikolai, who holds up his end of the bargain but advises her to keep the child in London, a much better place for it to grow up.

Semyon, recognising Stepan as an old KGB man, orders Nikolai to kill him. Nikolai makes the former agent vanish. Following Stepan's removal, Semyon's confidence in Nikolai grows. He sponsors him to become a full member of the gang. Nikolai is more competent than the dissolute and insecure Kirill, who he has been protecting against retaliation for indiscretions. Kirill, with the help of Azim, a Kurdish associate, had arranged the execution of a rival Chechen gang leader, who had spread rumours that Kirill was gay. This was the man killed in the barbershop, and his murderer was Azim's intellectually disabled nephew.

Nikolai's induction ritual requires him to stand almost naked before a panel of mafia grandees. In so doing, he exposes his tattoos, his identity, his story.

Welcomed into the 'family', Nikolai becomes untouchable. Kirill had forced him to rape a trafficked woman while he himself looked on, to prove that Nikolai was not gay. Now he bitterly accepts the other man's new status, knowing that his own power is slipping away.

Hitmen arrive in London. They kill Azim's nephew after a football match as the boy pisses on a headstone in a graveyard. Kirill realises that they're coming for him. The assassins have never seen Kirill, so when a meeting is arranged with Azim at a bathhouse, Semyon sends Nikolai instead.

At the meeting, Nikolai speaks with Azim. The hitmen enter the bathhouse and attack Nikolai, thinking him to be Kirill. The fight is intense, the assassins armed with knives. Naked, Nikolai wrestles with the men and manages to grab a knife. It's a carpet knife, which Nikolai swings like a claw, disabling then killing his assailants but not without cost. His wounds are severe and he is taken to hospital.

Following his recovery, Nikolai goes to a debriefing and is revealed as an agent of the FSB, working in Britain with the permission of the government. He has infiltrated Semyon's gang, which has meant his full participation in their criminal activities. Rape, murder, robbery, intimidation: he has done terrible things. Nikolai, allowed to read Tatiana's diary before the old man had it destroyed, knows what it contains. He arranges with his handler to have Semyon arrested for statutory rape. Thanks to Anna, he has the DNA evidence to prove the child's paternity. Later, he reassures Anna that her father is safe, sent to a five-star hotel in Edinburgh rather than murdered.

As a last attempt to protect himself, Semyon orders Kirill to steal Tatiana's child from the hospital and kill her. Kirill takes the baby to the place by the Thames where Nikolai and he would dump dead bodies. But he can't throw the child in. He needs to gather himself before committing such a crime. As he prevaricates, Nikolai and Anna arrive. They persuade him to hand over the baby, who is finally safe in the care of the kindly Anna. Like brothers, Nikolai and Kirill embrace. Semyon is finished and it's time for them to take over.

Installed in the Trans-Siberian as the new London head, Nikolai looks grimly to the future.

Comment

By the mid-2000s, in the dying days of New Labour, London had become a playground for oligarchs and international business. *Eastern Promises* follows the Russian mafia in the East End of the city, and the mobsters' effect on some of the people capitalism left behind. These gangsters, as in *The Godfather* or *Goodfellas*, are predators on their communities. Their story is an allegory of how, in today's societies, corporations may be let loose to operate as they please, and it is ordinary people who suffer. *Eastern Promises* is a heart-in-mouth experience, a morality play that shows us horrors every bit as appalling as anything in Cronenberg's more fantastical pictures. It's a believable account of what humans do to each other.

These mobsters are self-mythologising nihilists, with their arcane rituals, their storytelling tattoos, their codes of dishonour. They traffic women for sex but pray sincerely to a Christian god. The city is their manor, their dominance assumed. Into this world steps an innocent, Anna, whose primary impulse is to help others. This is clear to the gangsters she meets, who initially don't see her as a threat. Once she reveals that she has Tatiana's diary, mob boss Semyon's attitude to her changes. He turns like a vampire who spots a paper cut on a finger but must restrain himself, as the hand might hold a crucifix.

Everyone is dispensable here, even Semyon himself. There's a hierarchy, and threats come from below as well as from outside. Anna's good heart places her in danger. Naomi Watts makes us care very much what happens to her, but Anna is no Pollyanna. Real life is cruel, strange and horrific and she is determined to do what she can to make it better.

Nikolai, performed with sly menace by Viggo Mortensen, plays both sides of the fence because he needs to. If James Bond really existed, this is the kind of thug he would be: trapped, lost and doomed, on the side of the angels yet corrupted by his work so that he no longer belongs in polite company. In other words, he's a soldier in a war. One day Nikolai will be killed by some enemy or some friend. In the meantime, to do his job, he must tolerate the appalling Kirill, son of Semyon, the terrifying restaurateur. To protect his cover, Nikolai does not intervene when he sees women being abused, turned to prostitution, trafficked, and killed.

The fight scene at the bathhouse further exposes the brutality of this world. The hitmen's carpet knives heighten the horror of the attack. These claw-like weapons, scary just to look at, increase the tension and fear, accentuating the physical vulnerability of bare flesh against sharp metal. Mortensen decided not to hold on to his towel during the fight. Cronenberg told the *New York Times*: 'I used relatively wide lenses to see a lot of the bathhouse. I wanted to see full bodies, and it couldn't be impressionistic, but linear. So when I said to Viggo, "O.K., what are we going to do with the towel?" he said: "Well, I'm going to have to do it naked. It's obvious." And that was the end of the conversation.'

Mortensen, naked, plays Nikolai as defenceless as he can be, shading the fight with a muscular eroticism. This gladiatorial conflict comments on the gangsters' repressed sexuality. Kirill makes Nikolai rape a woman to prove that he is not gay, but his reaction suggests that he'd rather be watching two men. Repression fuels Kirill's nasty disposition and his intense attachment to drinking and fighting. He's paranoid and defensive, surviving in a culture in which to come out is to invite death. Machismo imprisons these men bound by their code, as it does men everywhere. When Anna and Nikolai find Kirill by the river, hesitating over killing the baby, he breaks. Kirill submits to the control which Nikolai disguises as partnership. His repression reasserts itself, and he finds a new place in the scheme of things, in league with his new 'brother'.

Tatiana's orphan is now Anna's to take care of. It's her reward, a gentle and powerful human connection, a note of hope in an otherwise grim world. This is in stark contrast with Nikolai's new situation. He rules in hell, waiting for the blade that will one day set him free.

A Dangerous Method (2011)

Production: Corus Entertainment, Dangerous Method Film AG, Deutscher Filmförderfonds, Elbe Film GmbH, Filmförderungsanstalt, Filmstiftung NRW, Lago Film GmbH, Media Programme of the European Union, Medienboard Berlin Brandenburg, Millbrook Pictures, MFG Filmförderung Baden-Württemberg, Movie Central, The Movie Network, Ontario Media Development Corporation, Prospero Pictures, Recorded Picture Company, RPC Danger Limited, Talking Cure Productions Limited, Telefilm Canada and the UK Film Council's Development Fund
Produced by Tiana Alexandra-Silliphant, Martin Katz, Stephan Mallmann, Richard Mansell, Marco Mehlitz, Karl Spoerri, Thomas Sterchi, Jeremy Thomas, Peter Watson and Matthias Zimmermann
Written by Christopher Hampton from his play and the novel by John Kerr
Cinematographer: Peter Suschitzky
Music: Howard Shore
Directed by David Cronenberg
Filming dates: 26 May to 24 July 2010
First Release: 2 September 2011, (Venice Film Festival)
Canada Release: September 2011 (TIFF), 13 January 2012 (general)
US release: 11 December 2011
UK release: 10 February 2012
Running time: 99 minutes
Budget: $14 million
Cast: Vincent Cassel (Otto Gross), Michael Fassbender (Carl Jung), Sarah Gadon (Emma Jung), Keira Knightley (Sabina Spielrein), Viggo Mortensen (Sigmund Freud)

Background

A Dangerous Method was originated by Christopher Hampton from his play *The Talking Cure*, itself based on *A Most Dangerous Method*, John Kerr's 1993 nonfiction examination of the relationship between Freud, Jung and Sabina Spielrein. The title comes from a letter that William James wrote to a colleague in 1910, describing the use of symbolism in psychoanalysis as 'a most dangerous method'.

In giving Spielrein her due, Kerr's book caused some upset, as it posited a new origin story for the field of psychoanalysis. It is rarely fun to have your backstory retconned, but such upheaval can reveal unexamined riches. Illuminating the dispute between Freud and Jung, the book gave ammunition to the anti-Freud faction. An essay based on Kerr's findings appeared in the *New York Review of Books*, prompting an unprecedented avalanche of letters to the publication. Producers picked Christopher Hampton to write a film of the story, with Julia Roberts proposed as Sabina. When talks stalled, Hampton adapted the material for theatre instead, and *The Talking Cure* opened in London, in 2003. Then producer Jeremy Thomas bought the rights to Hampton's play as well as his earlier screenplay and approached David Cronenberg to direct. This would be their third film together, after *Naked Lunch* and *Crash*.

Cronenberg had cast Christoph Waltz as Freud and was discussing the part of Jung with Christian Bale, but scheduling conflicts prevented their participation. Calling on his new muse Viggo Mortensen to play Freud, the director also cast Michael Fassbender as Jung and Keira Knightley as Sabina Spielrein. Vincent Cassel plays Otto, and Sarah Gadon is Emma, Jung's wife.

An international story with international funding, *A Dangerous Method* was shot over a two-month period in summer 2010, at locations in Vienna and Cologne, and at Lake Constance, which served as Lake Zurich's stunt double. The film debuted at the Venice Film Festival in September 2011 and began showing in the UK five months later. It was a moderate financial success.

Critics gave *A Dangerous Method* their approval, the film turning up on many 'best of the year' lists, although some found its detached tone too much. Roger Ebert called it 'absorbing' and noted the 'dialogue-heavy approach that's unusual for Cronenberg'.

Cronenberg was named Best Director at the Directors Guild of Canada Awards and at the Genies. Mortensen picked up awards for his supporting performance, and at the London Critics' Circle Film Awards, German-born Irish actor Michael Fassbender was named British Actor of the Year. Surely a Freudian slip.

Story

Sabina Spielrein, daughter of a rich Russian Jewish family, comes to the *Burghölzli*, the leading psychiatric hospital in Zurich. It is 1904, and Carl Jung, a young Swiss doctor, is using Freud's new science of psychoanalysis to treat patients. Sabina suffers from 'hysteria', a condition triggered by humiliation and sexual assault as a child: her father used to punish her by spanking her naked bottom. In Sabina's mind, she has been hearing the voice of a German-speaking angel telling her that she has done nothing wrong. It might be that she was the object of her father's redirected anger: Sabina's mother was unfaithful; her cuckolded husband took his rage out on their daughter instead. Her family's wealth allowed her to have a brilliant education before university, where she learned about everything except sex. Sabina is still a virgin when she comes to see Jung.

Soon into her stay at the hospital, the authorities recognise her intelligence and aptitude. Eugene Bleule, the head of the facility, together with Jung, decide that as Sabina intends to study medicine, they will take her on as an assistant. This work includes noting the physical reactions of patients during word-association tests, to build through empirical observation a scientific grounding for psychoanalysis. Jung wants to use scientific data to temper the absolutism of Freud's theories that all mental illness comes from sexual experiences in childhood, whether real or imagined. As well as watching the patients, Jung and his doctors study the behaviour of themselves and their families. This is a new field, hungry for experimental data and open to possibilities. Freud and Jung have yet to meet, although their mutual admiration is strong. They begin to analyse each other, sharing details of their dreams. In time, Freud sees Jung as his natural successor and makes him his agent.

Sabina, meanwhile, has prospered in her new role, becoming increasingly self-aware. Jung considers her a like-minded individual and admires her ability to see things differently. As he analyses her, Sabina develops signs of transference, becoming attracted to Jung, who reciprocates her attachment, to create a chain of affection and power. Jung intends to take his feelings for Sabina no further, as he is against infidelity to his wife Emma, and sleeping with a patient is unacceptable.

Otto Gross, a remorseless philanderer and brilliant psychoanalyst, becomes Jung's patient. Gross disapproves of monogamy and, suggesting that Jung's resistance to relations with Sabina is a symptom of repression, urges him to give in to his impulses.

Jung not only becomes Sabina's lover, with spanking and bondage in their repertoire, he oversees her dissertation. Now he is in the unusual situation of publishing his observations of her treatment, as well as her own work.

Spielrein is just as brilliant as the men. Her ideas blossom, fed by self-examination of her childhood abuse, as well as her complicated relationship with Jung, her mentor and new father figure. Her original insight is that to create; one must have a drive to destroy. Taboos must break, opposites must collide. This holds true not just in sexual desire but in all kinds of creative acts. One such act would be to have a child with an illicit lover. Sabina wants a baby, but Jung refuses her desire. Instead, he tries to return their relationship to simply that of doctor and patient.

Sabina is having none of it. She could have outed Jung and damaged his career but does not want to. Instead, she approaches Freud and forces Jung to tell him the truth.

On a trip to America, Jung and Freud begin to disagree about aspects of psychoanalysis. Though their professional respect continues, their friendship breaks down.

Back in Switzerland, while she works on her dissertation, Sabina and Jung rekindle their relationship, but he still refuses to leave his wife. Spielrein leaves him instead and goes to Vienna, where she meets Freud, whose ideas she prefers over Jung's. However, she believes that for psychoanalysis to have a future, the two men must reconcile: opposites coming together for the sake of the project. Their masculine posturing is harming the work, and Sabina's insights are proving more useful than theirs. Freud and Jung resume their correspondence as their disagreements grow more hostile.

After Freud collapses at a conference, he and Jung end their relationship. There is no bridging the gap between their competing concepts of psychoanalysis.

Sabina gets married and has a child with her Russian husband, a doctor. Visiting Jung and his wife, she learns not only that his love for her has made him a better person but that he has taken a new mistress.

Titles then reveal what happened to the characters. In 1919, Otto Gross died of starvation in Berlin. Driven out of Vienna by the Nazis, Sigmund Freud died of cancer in London in 1939. Sabina Spielrein went to the Soviet Union, where she trained analysts. In 1942, the Nazis shot her and her two daughters. Carl Jung had a nervous breakdown. He died quietly in 1961, renowned as the greatest psychologist in the world.

Comment

More clinically erotic than *Fifty Shades of Grey*, the novel that was then putting kink into commuting, *A Dangerous Method* is an elegant discussion of several themes that have lost none of their relevance. Repression, patriarchy, familial violence, and gender dynamics, are all here, driving the characters and their approach to psychiatry, which means that these people couldn't possibly have carried out their experiments in a sterile environment. It's early days, clearly, and the new discipline sometimes involves spanking.

The film shows its theatrical roots: it feels like a literary chamber piece, giving it the intimacy it needs. Although the *Quietus* wondered if it had 'too much analysis and not enough psycho', *A Dangerous Method* does take risks. A period movie, it appears to be not your father's Cronenberg, but in the same way that *M. Butterfly* dealt with identity, love and power, this story goes to the root of everything the director has been working on for decades. Freud and Jung are his household gods. Spielrein joins them as a not-so-holy ghost. Her affair with Jung, in the film, is one of those relationships where the participants watch each other having it, and take notes. Everything is material for the project. They're natural observers and they act like writers.

After his detour into violent crime, Cronenberg dives into recovery, showing how a parent's abuse may shape a child's journey into adulthood. He discusses the power that medical professionals can wield over their patients; and illustrates how the scientific curiosity of doctors can lead them to view the patient as less interesting than their condition. This chimes with themes in *Dead Ringers* and *The Brood*, for instance. Sabina is more than a catalyst for the dynamic between Freud and Jung, titans throwing lightning bolts. Their relationship begins through correspondence about her case, but she comes into her own, growing beyond the role of victim or subject. Furthermore, Sabina worries that the animosity between the men may endanger the field she is helping to invent. She claims part-ownership of the enterprise.

The horror in *A Dangerous Method* comes from within, as Cronenberg and his writer bring hidden desires into the light. Keira Knightley plays Sabina Spielrein with an intensity that she modulates expertly throughout, so that the power between the character and her hysteria gradually exchanges places. It is remarkable to watch as Sabina, incapacitated by trauma, opens herself to the world. By the end, Knightley convinces us that the 'hysteria' is still there, under the surface but also under control. Viggo Mortensen is quietly superb as Freud, who sees everyone as a potential case. Michael Fassbender is very good as Jung, a man of his time: romantic, patriarchal and self-important, compartmentalising his work, his home life, and his mistresses.

Peter Suschitzky's photography is cool and sumptuous at the same time. By incorporating a piano transcription of Wagner's *Siegfried Idyll* performed delicately by Lang Lang, the score hints at a troubled future for the characters.

How faithful is *A Dangerous Method*? The story, based in historical fact, makes artistic innovations in the service of the story. Cronenberg claimed the film to be 'perfectly accurate because it was from a letter-writing period... I can back up almost every line of dialogue with quotes from letters'. It is debatable whether Sabina and Jung had a sexual relationship in real life. From what Sabina writes to Freud (that she had given her 'maidenhood' and 'innocence' to Jung) Cronenberg believes that they did. In the film, their affair is 'an invention with justification'. Others disagree. In 2012, David Van Nuys PhD wrote in *Psychology Today*: 'There is no concrete evidence of their having had an affair, let alone the sadomasochistic elements so vividly portrayed in the movie'. He contends that although Cronenberg's research is thorough and his intention sincere, the director strives for artistic truth, which is not the same as fact; and that this risks reinforcing unhelpful stereotypes. It is true that many in the audience will not look further. It is also true that the film stands on its merits as a piece of art. Van Nuys makes a valuable point, and those who wish to explore the debate might read Kerr's book or watch other films on the subject, particularly Roberto Faenza's docudrama *The Soul Keeper* and Elisabeth Marton's *My Name Was Sabina Spielrein*, both from 2002.

A Dangerous Method came out in the same year as Tanya Wexler's film *Hysteria*, about how the Victorians invented the vibrator by mistake. The two films would make for an enjoyable evening of therapy.

Cosmopolis (2012)

Production: Alfama Films, Astral Media's The Harold Greenberg Fund, Canal+, Entertainment One, France 2 Cinéma, France Televisions, Jouror Productions, Kinologic Films (DC), Leopardo Filmes, Ontario Media Development Corporation, Prospero Pictures, Radiotelevisão Portuguesa (as RTP), Rai Cinema, Talandracas Pictures and Telefilm Canada
Produced by Paulo Branco, Edouard Carmignac, Manuel Castelo-Branco, Martin Katz, Pierre-Ange Le Pogam, Gregoire Melin, Renee Tab
Written by David Cronenberg from the novel by Don DeLillo
Cinematographer: Peter Suschitzky
Music: Howard Shore, Metric
Directed by David Cronenberg
Filming dates: 25 May to 24 July 2011
Canada release: 8 June 2012
US release: 17 August 2012
UK release: 15 June 2012
Running time: 109 minutes
Budget: $20.5 million
Cast: Abdul Ayoola (Ibrahim Hamadou), Juliette Binoche (Didi Fancher), Kevin Durand (Torval), Sarah Gadon (Elise Shifrin), Paul Giamatti (Benno Levin), Emily Hampshire (Jane Melman), Samantha Morton (Vija Kinsky), Robert Pattinson (Eric Packer)

Background

Cosmopolis followed hard on the heels of *A Dangerous Method*, though it had been in the works since February 2009, when *Screen Daily* announced that Paulo Branco's Alfama Films would be producing it. David Cronenberg was named that July as the director, with filming set for 2010. By September 2009, he had finished the screenplay, his first entirely self-written piece since *eXistenZ*.

Four months later, no actors were in place, or production schedule set. Colin Farrell had to leave because of a commitment to the *Total Recall* remake, so Robert Pattinson came on board as Eric Packer, the young man who loses his fortune in a day. Supporting players included Samantha Morton, Mathieu Almaric, Paul Giamatti, and Sarah Gadon. Juliette Binoche played Packer's art consultant, and would later star alongside Pattinson in Claire Denis's deranged and brilliant SF nightmare *High Life* (2018).

Filming took place in Toronto from May to July 2011. Locations included Yonge Street, Union Station on Front Street, and Stage 7 at Pinewood Toronto. Some background plates were shot in New York. Howard Shore collaborated with Metric, an indie band he'd worked with on *Twilight: Eclipse*. Shore and Metric won for best original score at the Canadian Screen Awards in 2013.

By coincidence, another limousine-based film, Leos Carax's *Holy Motors*, also came out in 2012. Carax's film is the fantastical counterpoint to Cronenberg's icy modernism. The films make fine, if unintentional, companion pieces.

It was to another story that critic Philip French looked when praising *Cosmopolis* in the Guardian. '... I was reminded of John Cheever's *New Yorker* short story, *The Swimmer* (filmed in 1968 starring Burt Lancaster) ... Cronenberg's film has a similar mordancy, though at the end – and probably deliberately – it doesn't touch the heart or elicit much compassion for the protagonist.'

Cosmopolis opened first in France, on 25 May at Cannes, where it was nominated for the Palme d'Or. As it rolled out elsewhere, the critical reception was both glowing and cool. It proved a difficult film to warm to. *The Hollywood Reporter* called it 'lifeless and stagey' but *Cahiers du Cinéma* chose it as their second-best film of the year. In the review quoted above, Philip French praised the film as 'riveting cinema, as fine as anything Cronenberg has done ... '

Yet another critical hit that didn't do well at the box office, *Cosmopolis* seemed to indicate that by now Cronenberg's films were becoming more prestigious than profitable. Then again, as Eric Packer might tell you, money isn't everything.

Story

'We need a haircut,' Eric Packer says to his driver, Ibrahim, as they wait at a line of limousines, one of them his. A 28-year-old asset manager, Eric's rise has been meteoric and he's already a billionaire. Today he wants to get his haircut from an old barber on the other side of Manhattan. His stretch limousine, a luxury high-tech mobile office and mogul-cocoon, is soon stuck in traffic. The space it takes up further slows it to the pace of gridlock. Ibrahim does his best, frustrated at Eric's refusal to use a local barber or to have one come to the car. Crossing town, the driver warns, will be a nightmare. The President is here on a visit, protesters are clogging the streets, and the world's biggest Sufi rap artist has died, his funeral adding to the congestion.

As if his day couldn't get any worse, Eric's security chief Torval, walking with his detail alongside the limousine, reports that 'the complex' has identified a 'credible threat'. Turning on the television, Eric watches a report of a businessman brutally attacked on a news programme. This incident has sparked an unexpected surge in the value of the yuan, against which Eric has invested. The exchange rate starts to rise remorselessly, threatening to wipe out the value of his investments. By the end of the day, he will no longer have a personal fortune and will have lost billions for his clients.

While Eric's mistress Didi Fancher visits him in the car for sex, he speculates about buying the Rothko Chapel with its fourteen black paintings. Didi disapproves of his lack of respect for a building that should belong to the world. She'd understand if he wanted to buy a single Rothko, but the entire Chapel? He nonetheless instructs her to make enquiries.

While receiving a prostate exam from his doctor, Eric carries on a conversation with Jane Melman, his chief of finance, who had been on her day off until he called her. The doctor discovers that Eric has an asymmetric prostate, another worrying new fact.

Eric meets his wife Elise, who is a poet and an heiress, in a café. He brings up the subject of sex, arguing that they shouldn't waste time not having it. Elise says she smells sex on him now, but he retorts that what she smells is hunger.

In the limo again, his 'chief of theory', Vija Kinsky, discusses the nature of time, its infinite divisibility, and the effect that has on what we call the present moment. The present moment is something that hardly exists.

It becomes clear as Eric meets Elise again at various stops on his journey, that their three-week-old marriage is mostly sexless. It is, as Didi observed earlier, a marriage of convenience designed to bring two large fortunes together. When Eric suggests it, Elise refuses to have sex with him in a hotel. He compensates by going to the hotel anyway and having sex with Kendra, one of his bodyguards, getting her to taser him so that he can feel what it's like.

Protesters attack the car, not knowing who's inside. Eric meets Elise in a diner, when a protester rushes in, holding a pair of rats and calling out 'A spectre is haunting the world!' before throwing the rodents at the patrons then running away. The spectre is capitalism, in a twist on Karl Marx, for whom it was communism.

Rats are currency, remembers Eric from a poem. According to him, the anarchists believe that 'the urge to destroy is a creative urge'. He seems to believe the same and is acutely aware that he now has problems. Trading has continued to wipe the value from his clients' investments, and Eric's personal wealth is evaporating. He meets Elise again outside a theatre where she stands, having left at the intermission. She's smoking a cigarette, which surprises him.

At dinner, they try to impress each other with the effort they're making to connect. Elise says she doesn't know how to do this, to be indifferent. He tells her that his company's portfolio and his personal fortune are running down to nothing and that there's a threat to his life. It all makes him feel free. 'Free to do what? Go broke and die?' she asks. Elise promises to look after him financially but decides that their marriage is over. In a club with Ibrahim, Eric discusses the young people and their dancing, and the pain they must feel. There is plenty of pain to go around.

Back in the limousine, Eric gets an update from Torval. They're trying to pin down the threat that is still out there.

A man enters the car and informs Eric of the death of Fez the rapper. Eric is crestfallen. He loved Fez and played his music in one of his elevators. The man criticises the state of the limo's exterior, which is now covered in paint from the protests. He hopes that Eric isn't disappointed that Fez died of natural causes.

The car stops again on the way to the barbershop. A performance artist called André, known as the Pastry Assassin, hits Eric with a pie in the face. Torval detains the man as Eric kicks him while paparazzi swarm around, taking shots. André calls himself an artist of the creamed pie and claims that he creamed Fidel Castro several times. No doubt.

Standing with Torval by a basketball court before proceeding to the barber, Eric discusses the continued threat to his life. The man who is coming will be armed, and Torval, also armed, will have to shoot him. The men banter and appear to be striking up a rapport. Eric asks Torval for his gun; he complies. The weapon is voice-activated and protected by a code, which Eric gets Torval to speak. Then he shoots his security chief dead. A couple of kids playing basketball look on as Eric tosses the weapon into their court.

Pissing in the car, Packer seems to have gone over the edge. His driver opens the door and announces that they have arrived. It is then shown that Eric is urinating into a retractable toilet bowl.

It's late evening when they arrive at the barbershop, which is closed, but the barber, Anthony, opens for Eric. As they speak, it's revealed that Anthony not only used to cut Eric's hair, he used to cut his father's too. Eric's father died when the boy was four or five. It's been a long time. Anthony offers him food, some takeaway from the fridge. Eric invites Ibrahim to join him. While Anthony cuts Eric's hair, he exchanges reminiscences with Ibrahim of driving cabs in New York years before. Ibrahim was a high-ranking politician in his old country until a coup forced him to come to the United States as a political refugee, where he ended up driving for a living.

Ibrahim remarks that Torval is not with them. Eric tells him that he gave the security chief the night off. Realising that Eric is unarmed and unprotected, Anthony gives him his own gun and Eric decides to leave with only half a haircut. Ibrahim goes with him.

The two men ride in the front of the limo now, and Ibrahim drives it to the garage, after which he will take his own car home to New Jersey. Eric and Ibrahim embrace and say goodbye. Then Eric takes the gun and walks across the road from the garage. There's somewhere he needs to be.

In a rundown apartment, he finds his potential assassin, Benno Levin, a former employee also known as Richard Sheets. Eric doesn't remember him, but he listens as Sheets tells him how being fired destroyed his life. Sheets was cut loose by the capitalist system. He blames Eric for seeking symmetry in the markets; when something asymmetric happened, as his body via the prostate was trying to warn him, he was unprepared, hence his downfall. Eric, holding Anthony's gun, seems about to kill himself but shoots his hand instead. Sheets takes the gun and points it at Eric. The film cuts to black.

Comment

This bleak satire of capitalism after the crash of 2008 – though the novel is set immediately post 9-11 – casts a very cold eye indeed. Pattinson is great as Eric Packer in an existentially fraught film that's also intensely political. *Cosmopolis*, which is clearly on the side of the 99%, gets more meditative as it goes along until it bursts into unspeakable violence. The cameos help shed light on Eric's character, his anger held in check beneath a calm, apparently indifferent exterior. He is the weakly shining sun around which his visitors orbit. Once he goes, they will fall into the darkness left by his absence. He is, in fact, America, or the part of it that lives on Broad Street, Manhattan.

The shooting and blocking here is masterful. Within the confines of the limousine set, a world unfolds and never feels more claustrophobic than it has to be. The staging allows for a sense of space that grows with the needs of the story, where great themes of life and death, control and release, the power of money and the oppression that poverty attracts, all play out in an inversion of perspective where real life is kept outside the door. The space, therefore, suits the tone of a film that some found icy. *Cosmopolis* is a dream of unease and disquiet, of a man melting down because of how cold his life is. Protected by money and privilege from a world that's exploding, his only escape is to throw himself and his fortune away. Cronenberg's last straightforward literary adaptation, the book is less unfilmable than its reputation suggests, and certainly a lot easier to imagine as a movie than *Crash* or *Naked Lunch* had been. The restricted setting is Pinteresque. It also reminds us of a vogue some years ago for 'theatre in a car', where the audience, all two of them, would sit in the back seat while a pair of actors played out a drama in the front. *Cosmopolis* is that, but on acid.

Cronenberg adapted Don De Lillo's novel in six days, at stream-of-consciousness speed, transcribing the dialogue into screenplay format and adding stage directions. His intention was to keep as much of DeLillo's speech as possible, and its artifice, when spoken aloud, helps to distance the characters from each other, from the world outside, from the viewer. Adding to that chilling effect, this was the first Cronenberg picture not shot on film. Its digital nature matches Eric's alienation perfectly, as Pattinson gives his best performance up until then, using facial expressions sparingly as if the value of emotions may fall as well as rise. That there are so few of them is revealing. Eric doesn't know what he feels but does know what he wants. Addicted to technology and sex, money and power, he is a sham, his marriage a charade, and when he loses his money, he loses his wife. An old axiom has it that, 'when money goes out the door, love flies out the window,' except that here there is no love to begin with, and soon there will be no door, no window.

Can Eric be redeemed? Facing a death that he has pursued all day, the certainty of it liberates him to commit atrocities against innocent people and against himself, just to find out how it feels to transgress so deliberately. He is becoming human at last but in the most horrific way.

The direction of travel in Eric's limousine is all the way to the end. His visitors are a gallery of colleagues, dependents, emotional cripples, and medical professionals, all peddling epigrammatic trivia on important subjects. In a hilarious parody of how a busy executive might show off his ability to multitask, Eric submits to digital penetration during the prostate exam, while holding a conversation with one of his advisers, a woman who is not phased by Eric's display, but resents him for having disrupted her day off.

Is there any love in this limo, as there isn't in his marriage? Hardly. All the love is outside, dancing with hate. Eric goes on like Macbeth steeped in blood. At Sheets' apartment, he stands in front of a man who was an abstraction, a

115

man whose life he has destroyed. It's irrelevant, this life, as is Eric's imminent death. He knows now that he is human, and that he has worked and lived mainly in the abstract. When the screen goes black, we are left to speculate as he himself has always done, unaware of who has been hurt. If he dies, he does so without feeling the bullet. Is the gun even fired?

Eric Packer was a young man, no longer in a hurry. All he wanted was a haircut.

Maps to the Stars (2014)

Production: Prospero Pictures, SBS Productions. Distribution; Entertainment One Films (Canada), Le Pacte (France), MFA+ Filmdistribution (Germany), Focus World (US)
Produced by Saïd Ben Saïd, Martin Katz, Michel Merkt. Written by Bruce Wagner
Cinematographer: Peter Suschitzky
Music: Howard Shore
Directed by David Cronenberg
Filming dates: July to August 2013
Canada release: 9 September 2014 (TIFF)
US release: 27 September 2014 (New York Film Festival)
UK release: 26 September 2014
Running time: Running time 111 minutes
Budget: $13 million
Cast: Evan Bird (Benjie Weiss), John Cusack (Stafford Weiss), Sarah Gadon (Clarice Taggart), Julianne Moore (Havana Segrand), Robert Pattinson (Jerome Fontana), Mia Wasikowska (Agatha Weiss), Olivia Williams (Cristina Weiss)

Background

In a 2015 interview with *Film Comment*, David Cronenberg was asked about possible links between the siblings in *Maps to the Stars* and those in *Dead Ringers*, in that they're damned from the start. He remarked of both pairs that they '... committed gentle suicide at the end. Yeah, that's definitely a connection'. The connection is unintentional, he said, as Bruce Wagner had written the script 'about 20 years ago', and he himself had read it 'about 10 years ago'. They had made quite a few attempts to get the film off the ground since then, as either an American production or a Canadian co-production. By the time Cronenberg took *Cosmopolis* to Cannes in 2012, Wagner had already been working on *Maps to the Stars*, on and off, for seventeen years. Still it evolved, the director and writer trimming the screenplay to make it leaner. Along the way, certain cultural changes in society meant alterations: cellphones weren't common when the early drafts were written, so the script was updated to include them. Now-irrelevant pop culture references were removed or replaced. Aside from keeping the screenplay current, said Cronenberg, the dialogue hadn't changed much at all, and the central family dynamic remained the same from one draft to the next. Despite having a well-honed story by now, the film was no further along when Wagner wrote a blistering, satirical novel called *Dead Stars*, based on the screenplay.

At Cannes with *Cosmopolis*, the director said he was still unsure as to whether he could get *Maps to the Stars* made even now, as it was a 'hard sell'. What finally sold it was the casting of Robert Pattinson. His presence would be the strongest commercial element in what the director considered a non-Hollywood picture.

In his second collaboration with David Cronenberg, Pattinson plays a limousine driver, switching seats after the last time. The key character is played by Mia Wasikowska, first among equals in a fine ensemble that also includes Julianne Moore, Sarah Gadon, John Cusack, Olivia Williams and Evan Bird. Viggo Mortensen had been in line to play Stafford, the role that Cusack eventually took. Rachel Weisz would have been Havana.

Production ran from July to August 2013, with five days of filming around Los Angeles: in Hollywood, Beverly Hills, the Chateau Marmont for the scene with Carrie Fisher, and the children's hospital on Sunset, where Benjie visits his ailing fan. This was Cronenberg's first time filming actual scenes in the United States. He had often wanted to shoot there, but the value of the Canadian dollar relative to the US currency meant that American producers found it more cost-effective for him to film in Hollywood North. He now found the resonance of shooting in L.A., 'the heart of darkness', both cathartic and satisfying.

The crew also filmed for 24 days on location and on soundstages in Toronto. The film's photography is bold and colourful, yet the shots are still, unshowy, putting the focus on the characters' emotions and how they move in their natural habitat. It's practically a *Discovery* exposé on celebrity animals. This is Peter Suschitzky's eleventh feature with Cronenberg, and both have won several Genie awards. It's therefore tempting to wonder whether Agatha's use of a Genie rather than an Oscar to kill Havana is a reference to something being out of the bottle, or simply a Canadian stamp on the film.

On 25 July 2014, *Maps to the Stars* opened in the Legends section of the New Zealand International Film Festival. It screened as a gala presentation at Toronto on 9 September before showings in New York, the UK, Tokyo, and Canada. To qualify for awards, the film hit L.A. in December and entered a wider US release two months later.

Most of the notices were positive, though there were reservations. Peter Bradshaw's approving review in *The Guardian* called the film a 'gripping and exquisitely horrible movie' that is 'positively vivisectional in its sadism and scorn'.

On the other hand, Anthony Lane in the *New Yorker* was less impressed by 'the guy who made *The Fly*' turning up in Hollywood and shooting on Rodeo Drive. 'As a portrait of the movie industry, *Maps to the Stars* pales beside the fire of a film like Robert Aldrich's *The Big Knife*, from sixty years ago...' He does allow that the film is 'at its most potent and beautiful by far when it becomes a ghost story – when the departed, not just Havana's mother, return to quiz the living'.

Maps to the Stars lost money at the box office, despite Pattinson's presence. Maybe it was just too much of a 'brilliant nightmare' as *The Guardian* said. A last word goes to Nathan Lee in *Film Comment*, who observed: 'A "map to the stars" can be two different things: a tacky accessory of celebrity culture, or a diagram of cosmic energy'.

Story

Maps to the Stars opens with a quotation from Paul Éluard's 'Liberté'. Lines from the poem will recur as a motif throughout the film. After this title card, the film cuts to another lovely day at LAX, where a young woman, Agatha, hires a limo to take her to the former home of Benjie Weiss, child star. Along the way, we see that Agatha has serious burns to her face, she wears long black gloves to hide her hands and forearms, and she takes medication. The limo driver, Jerome, brings her to the site where the house burned down. Benjie doesn't live here anymore.

In fact, right at that moment, he's visiting a fan in hospital, a little girl suffering from non-Hodgkin's lymphoma. Benjie isn't sure what that is. As he speaks with the child, he seems to lack a certain empathy. Does he even know what that word, if he heard it, might mean? He's using this visit as a photo opportunity for publicity purposes. Sometime after this encounter, the girl passes away.

Benjie's father is Stafford Weiss, a TV psychologist. He's treating the actress Havana Segrand for trauma, his methods very tactile. Havana's mother, also a famous actress, emotionally abused her as a child. Now Havana wants to play the role her mother once had, in a remake of the film *Stolen Waters*. Her mother may be dead, but to Havana, the past isn't even the past. Much to Havana's chagrin, her agent has been finding it hard to get her the role. Meanwhile, Havana suffers visitations from a young version of her mother. A hallucination? A ghost?

Back with Benjie Weiss, whose mother is his handler. They're taking a meeting where they try to convince studio executives to give Benjie a film role, his comeback after drug rehab. He's only a child with much learning to do, and he'll be good this time.

Meeting her at the Chateau Marmont, Carrie Fisher suggests that Havana hire Agatha as her P.A., her 'chore whore'. Fisher and Agatha have got to know each other on social media, and Havana agrees. She soon gets the part she wanted in the *Stolen Waters* remake.

Agatha, now working for Havana, becomes established in Tinseltown. She dates Jerome, who at first is less into it than she is, but a romance soon grows.

Stafford Weiss, during a therapy session with Havana, learns that Agatha is in town. Agatha's surname is also Weiss. She is the daughter of Stafford and Cristina, and they don't want anything to do with her.

Agatha has other ideas. Because she works for Havana, she gains entry to the production lot and goes to visit Benjie in his trailer.

Revealed as schizophrenic, Agatha tells Benjie that she has returned from the sanatorium. She wants only to make amends for burning down the house and nearly killing him. Benjie seems phlegmatic about her return. For their parents, it's a different matter. When Stafford learns that Agatha has come to see Benjie, he visits her and demands angrily that she leave town.

Disaster strikes. While visiting his only friend, Benjie gets high, ending his sobriety. Out of his head, Benjie shoots his friend's dog. The dog dies whimpering.

Now, Agatha goes to see her mother, Cristina, who tells her that she and Stafford are brother and sister. They did not know this at the time they had their children. Agatha waits for Stafford to come home, then tells him she knows that her parents are siblings. Angered by her discovery, Stafford beats Agatha severely until Cristina stops him. In the confusion, Agatha steals her mother's wedding ring.

Between takes on his comeback film, Benjie hangs out on set with his co-star, a younger child actor whose success Benjie resents. Hallucinating the girl that he met in hospital, a delirious Benjie tries to kill her. Instead, he strangles his co-star, who survives. Benjie will now be replaced on the shoot. He's out, forever.

Havana, who knows about Jerome and Agatha's relationship, hires him to drive her. When he arrives, she gets in the car and seduces him. Agatha sees them from a window of the house, her boss and her boyfriend having sex. Afterwards, Havana returns to the house and criticises Agatha's performance at work. Agatha gets up from Havana's opulent white couch, revealing that she has stained it with her menstrual blood. Furious, Havana insults and humiliates Agatha, who attacks her by hitting her across the back of the head with a film award. Havana Segrand, like her mother, is a dead star.

Stafford gets home to find Cristina by the swimming pool. She's engulfed in flames. The sight of her burning to death shatters him.

That night Benjie also comes home. Finding Stafford catatonic, he steals his father's wedding ring and leaves the house.

Returning to where their story began, Benjie meets Agatha at the site of their old house. Sitting in the ruins, the siblings, who are also cousins, exchange their parents' rings and 'marry' each other. Then they each take a large dose of Agatha's medication, intending to commit suicide. Lying back on the ground amid the scorched remains of their childhood, the pair of damaged children look up to the stars that will fade before their eyes in a slow dissolve to nothing.

Comment

For David Cronenberg, *Maps to the Stars* was not so much a dissection of Hollywood types as a psychologically realistic drama. After its release, he told Matt Hoffman at *Scene Creek*, 'I knew when I read Bruce's script that this was true. That this is not a satire: this is reality.' The story could happen anywhere. At its core is a tale of family horror and abuse. *The Brood* is in there somewhere, with therapist-guru Stafford Weiss and his manipulation of Havana Segrand recalling one of Cronenberg's renegade doctors. The offspring Stafford creates with his wife in their tainted couplings are this film's rage babies. The humour that *Maps to the Stars* needs, and with which it is riddled, is laughter in the dark.

Havana is brittle and hard but also ridiculous, hilarious, and nasty. A woman-child abandoned by her mother for the life of the actress, Havana's issues, underlined by Carrie Fisher's cameo, are the kind that you don't get over. Poisoned by her dragon-mother, Havana has been dying from that toxin since puberty.

Benjie is a child star about to throw his future away on drugs and despair, and he doesn't seem to have any feeling about it one way or another. Inside, he's as scared as the rest of them.

Stafford and Cristina are cracked and dangerous, hallucinatory in their denial, terrified that their world will crash around them if the truth is revealed. Their daughter burned the house down when she left. If she returns, will she torch what survived?

It is Cristina who starts the second fire, causing Stafford, faced with consequences, to disappear inside his mind. There is no *kintsugi* for that kind of fracture.

Havana gets what she wants, her mother's old role, but she will never have her mother's approval. When Agatha bashes her skull in with an award, it's a mercy killing.

Death is the solution. For Agatha and Benjie, it's the only way out.

The actors are fearless. Julianne Moore delights us with her commitment. The scene where Havana goes to the toilet with the door open while she holds a conversation with Agatha, is not only naturalistic to the point of hilarity, it illustrates the boundary issues neither character sees in herself. Moore sells it without inviting prurience.

John Cusack, at the top of his game, gets his teeth into Stafford as a New Age bullshit-artist, frightening and contemptible rather than pitiable. Robert Pattinson is good value as the driver, sleazy like the rest of them, just trying to get ahead. Evan Bird is a real find, playing Benjie as an emotionally malformed child-monster. Bird's only previous film was Jennifer Lynch's *Chained*. Cusack, impressed by his performance in *Maps*, warned him against becoming Benjie in real life.

Mia Wasikowska is the star of this show, with a playful and serious portrayal of Agatha, the broken child, the catalyst, the detonator of her nuclear family. She is the prism through which the light and shade of others is exposed, and she manipulates them all to get what she wants. Like Joe in *A History of Violence*, Agatha is the ghost who comes back. So too is Cristina, Havana's film-star mother, who haunts her daughter in a waking dream. *Maps to the Stars* is full of these ghosts. It is rotten with phantoms, as befits a film about Hollywood, a town obsessed with its own past, its own glories, the dead stars who haunt the boulevards, their names underfoot.

As Agatha and Benjie respond to each other like the notes of the story's heartbeat, the demonic soap operas of David Lynch's Los Angeles come to mind, but that is too easy. *Maps to the Stars* goes back to *Sunset Boulevard* and *All About Eve*, to Joan Didion's *Play it as it Lays*, to Michael Tolkin and

Robert Altman's *The Player*. Asserting that his film is not particularly a satire of Hollywood, the director says in the interview with *Scene Creek*, 'Any human endeavour has those aspects'. On the surface, it does work as a scabrous Hollywood takedown, but its depths are more treacherous. It is one of the least forgiving pictures that Cronenberg has made, and that is a compliment. At the end of his seventh decade, he is still taking risks and making bold choices. If *Maps to the Stars* is to be the last movie he directs, it caps the so-called Cronenberg canon in wild style.

Later Short Films

Camera (2000)

Production: Astral Media, The Movie Network, Super Écran
Produced by Niv Fichman, Jody Shapiro, Jennifer Weiss
Cinematographer: André Pienaar
Written and directed by David Cronenberg
Running time: 6 minutes
Cast: Les Carlson (as the actor); Marc Donato, Kyle Kassardjian, Natasha La Force, Katie Lai, Harrison Kane, Daniel Magder, Chloe Reis, Camille Shniffer (as the children), the Panavision camera (as itself)

Background

Camera was commissioned as one of the *Preludes* for the Toronto International Film Festival, 25th Anniversary.

Story

While being filmed on a video camera as he sits in his kitchen, a veteran actor discusses the state of cinema and his life. The children have brought home a different camera, a huge old Panavision. Where they found it, who knows. They seem very excited, the actor says. We hear his ruminations as the children go to bring the camera in. 'Photography is death.'

The actor tells us that although he continues to act sporadically, his best days are behind him. He relates a dream he had before he became an actor: he was in a cinema watching a movie when he started ageing rapidly, the movie having given him a disease that brought him closer to death. And now, he tells us, the dream is coming true. He doesn't know how the kids have learned to work the Panavision camera, itself an obsolete machine approaching death – a camera with which he now begins to empathise.

Having been prepping the shoot, several of the children push the big camera into the room where the actor sits, and they get him ready for filming.

A clapperboard is cracked. One of the kids calls action.

We see the actor now in high-grade Panavision, under the gaze of his replacements. He begins again, repeating the lines he spoke at the start of the film. His eyes betray the sadness he feels at his imminent demise.

Comment

Camera is a lamentation for how cinema seems to be dying. It is also a compassionate meditation on ageing, and on the fact that our replacement is inevitable. Though we may hope for posterity to smile on us, posterity has other ideas. For all that, in *Camera* there seems to be a mutual respect between the generations even as the actor fears that his time is over. Les Carlson appears in his final role for David Cronenberg.

At the Suicide of the Last Jew in the World in the Last Cinema in the World (2007)
Written and directed by David Cronenberg
Collaborators: John Bannister, Deirdre Bowen, Brandon Cronenberg, Howard Shore, Carolyn Zeifman
Running time: 4 minutes
Cast: Gina Clayton (Sherry), Jesse Collins (Rob), David Cronenberg (Last Jew)

Background
This is a segment of *Chacun son cinéma*, a portmanteau film celebrating the 60th anniversary of the Cannes Film Festival. The feature comprises thirty-four three-minute films, directed by auteurs from around the world. It was part of a trend of such films at the time.

Story
Cronenberg plays a Jewish man who waits in the restroom of the last cinema on Earth. Once owned by a Jewish family, the theatre has since fallen into disrepair, so that the man can't sit out in the stalls. Over the course of the film, he loads a gun. Then he puts it in his mouth. A camera inside the restroom films these events for a television audience, as commentators discuss the end of cinema and of Jewishness while seeming not to mind that either is about to die.

Comment
Cronenberg's piece is a satire on the death of film, which makes it perfect for a commission to celebrate Cannes. A kind of *Purim spiel*, *At the Suicide...* reflects on the director's Jewish cultural identity and is a response to Hezbollah's mission statement to, as he said, 'kill every Jew in the world wherever they are'. The film observes the fact that history forgets not only the atrocities of the past, but the culture. Its birdbrain television commentators neither know nor care about what is lost.

The Nest (2013)
Written and directed by David Cronenberg
Running time: 10 minutes
Cast: Évelyne Brochu (Celestine), David Cronenberg (Molnar)

Background
Made to promote David Cronenberg's novel *Consumed*, this short film features characters from the book. It's shot in a handheld style on GoPro, to echo the technology used by the novel's protagonists. A two-minute cut was also used as a trailer for the book.

Story
Molnar, a plastic surgeon, interviews his patient, Celestine. She believes that

a nest of insects is growing inside her left breast and tries to convince him to perform a mastectomy. He is prepared to operate but says, 'I'm happy to remove your breast, it's just that I'm not sure how to handle the insects.' Eventually, he agrees to remove the breast, having been convinced by examining her with a stethoscope, that there really are insects in the 'nest'.

Comment

This is a slight return to the style and themes of earlier work. *The Nest* looks like it was filmed in someone's garage. It shows Molnar as another rogue doctor outside of normal society, a man whose dubious ethics enable the destructive impulses of a damaged patient. A joke about the doctor-patient relationship, plastic surgery, and the director's own predilection for unusual infestations of the human body and mind, *The Nest* is both funny and horrifying.

The Novel

Consumed (2014)

Scribner, 2014. 308 pages. ISBN 978-1-4165-9614-1

In David Cronenberg's career, literature and film are entwined. As we have seen, among his heroes were Burroughs and Nabokov. A literature graduate, he had expected to become a writer, so it now seems natural that his career evolved to embrace that ambition with *Consumed*.

As well as creating original works, Cronenberg translated other people's books into film, but like any good adapter, he knew that the film should not be a cover version. Creative destruction of the original is the point: to create something beautiful and new, related but not the same.

Consumed evolved out of a screenplay. It's a tale of techno-fetishist photographers chasing down the story of a couple of neo-Marxist philosophers who resemble a Sartre and de Beauvoir for our times. The book's ingredients include illicit plastic surgery, iPhone pornography, consumerism (of course) and a global conspiracy.

The novel's gestation period was long, thanks in part to its writer's need to put it aside when making films. At one point, his editors at Scribner were worried enough to almost cancel the contract, but they gave him an extension. Once he'd finished on *Cosmopolis*, Cronenberg focused on the book and finally delivered the manuscript. He has described directing the characters in the novel as he would move the actors on a shoot.

David Cronenberg had made books before: published scripts, the graphic novel of *eXistenZ*, and the art-book of *Red Cars*, but no literary novels. Influenced by Bruce Wagner's style, with *Consumed*, Cronenberg said that they were working 'out of the same zeitgeist'. As to whether the experience of writing fiction would affect how he would approach his next film, he told the *Daily Beast* in 2014: 'I doubt it. I don't really think it's transmissible. ... I don't think it translates, either way, they're pretty separate acts, other than that in each case you're being a dramatist, dealing with characters and narrative. If I were to write another screenplay, I wouldn't be thinking about novelistic techniques.'

That said, *Consumed* delivers 'essence of Cronenberg' and readers may come away feeling that they have seen his latest picture, stylised dialogue and all.

Appendices
Acting Director

David Cronenberg has had a parallel career as an actor, making appearances in several productions over the years, including his own. In *Shivers*, he plays the man thrusting his arm through a door as the horde chases Roger St. Luc down a corridor. He stands in as Max Renn wearing the helmet in *Videodrome*. He's the gynaecologist in Veronica's dream in *The Fly*, and an obstetrician in *Dead Ringers*. He takes an uncredited voice role as an auto-wreck salesman in *Crash*. In his short films, he's the lead in *At the Suicide of the Last Jew in the World in the Last Cinema in the World*, and plays the mostly offscreen Dr Molnar in *The Nest*.

He has also performed in work by other directors. These include: John Landis's *Into the Night* (1985) and *The Stupids* (1996), Clive Barker's *Nightbreed* (1990), Heywood Gould's *Trial By Jury*, Nicholas Campbell's *Boozecan*, Gary Ledbetter's *Henry & Verlin* (all 1994), Holly Dale's *Blood and Donuts*, Gus Van Sant's *To Die For* (both 1995), Michael Apted's *Extreme Measures* (1996), Don McKellar's short film *Blue* (1992), McKellar's feature film *Last Night* (1998), Gérard L'Écuyer's *The Grace of God* (1998), Russell Mulcahy's *Resurrection* (1999), sometime Cronenberg VFX supervisor Jim Isaac's entry in the *Friday the 13th* franchise, *Jason X* (2002), and Richard J. Lewis' *Barney's Version* (2010).

His acting for television includes roles in: *Moonshine Highway* (TV film, 1996), *The Newsroom* ('Meltdown: Part 1', as himself, 1997), *The Judge* (2001), *Alias* ('Remnants' and 'Conscious', 2003), *Happy Town* ('Polly Wants a Crack at Her', 2010), and *Rewind* (TV film, 2013).

In a canny piece of casting, Cronenberg narrated Ric Esther Bienstock's 2013 documentary *Tales from the Organ Trade*. He has also performed voice roles in Maxwell McCabe-Lokos' short film *Ape Sodom* (2016), and in the animated show *Pig Goat Banana Cricket* ('The Goofy Turkey Zone', as Dr Cronenbird, 2017).

More recently he played G. O. D. in Geordie Sabbagh's 2017 short film *Tomorrow's Shadows*. In Mary Harron's fine television adaptation of Margaret Atwood's *Alias Grace* (2017), Cronenberg portrays Reverend Verrenger. He is Walter in Albert Shin's *Disappearance at Clifton Hill* (2019), and a proctologist in Viggo Mortensen's debut as a director, *Falling* (2020), a film in which cinema legend Lance Henriksen gives the performance of his career. Perhaps his most unexpected acting job is a recurring role as Kovich, a Federation operative in *Star Trek: Discovery* (various episodes, 2020 onwards). His cool, understated performance is a welcome surprise in a show not known for them.

Cathode Ray Missions: Work for Television

Throughout his career, David Cronenberg has directed for television as well as cinema, beginning with short documentary fillers made in the early 1970s. He began helming episodes of TV around this time and continued to do so until the 1990s. Two of his television episodes work as short films in their own right: 'The Italian Machine', an episode of *Teleplay*, which he wrote as well as directed; and 'Secret Weapons', for *Programme X*.

Short documentaries
Cronenberg writes, shoots, edits, produces and directs.

1971
Letter from Michelangelo (5 minutes)
Jim Ritchie, Sculptor (6 minutes)
Tourettes (3 minutes)

1972
Fort York (8 minutes)
Don Valley (6 minutes)
Lakeshore (6 minutes)
Winter Garden (3 minutes)
Scarborough Bluffs (5 minutes)
In the Dirt (5 minutes)

TV series – episodes
1972
Programme X, CBC
Episode: 'Secret Weapons' (22 minutes)
Written by Norman Snider. Cast includes Ronald Mlodzik. A narrator tells us 'you are looking at film shot in 1977 during the civil war'. A scientist has made a performance-enhancing 'meta-adrenalin' that can stimulate calculated aggression in reluctant troops, but will he give it to the government or to the rebels?

1975
Peep Show, CBC
Episodes: 'The Victim' (23 minutes), 'The Lie Chair' (23 minutes)

1976
Teleplay, CBC
Episode: 'The Italian Machine' (22 minutes)
Cronenberg both writes and directs this tale of motorbike enthusiasts and their attempt to steal a rare Ducati 900 Desmo SuperSport from a rich man. The cylinder and cylinder head of Cronenberg's own Ducati inspired the telepod design in *The Fly*.

1988
Friday the 13th The Series (Paramount Television)
Episode: 'Faith Healer' (26 minutes)

1990
Scales of Justice
Episodes: 'Regina Versus Horvath' (47 minutes), 'Regina Versus Logan' (44 minutes)

Commericals
In 1989–90, David Cronenberg helmed some commercials. His four spots for Ontario Hydro share a crisp and efficient shooting style, as befits a series promoting energy conservation.

For Cadbury's Caramilk, he directed two commercials in which 'dream noir' spy scenarios play out, with the secret of Caramilk as the McGuffin. The style is Cronenberg-lite.

Industrial Light and Magic developed a series of four commercials for Nike, each filmed by a different director. Cronenberg's 'Transformation' reflects his freaky side. A man uses a wheelbarrow to carry what look like larvae, through a field of pods that resemble Giger's alien eggs. A claw from one of the pods grabs a larva, takes it inside and incubates it, revealing a Nike Air 180 running shoe. The shoe transforms the larva into an athlete, who bursts out of the egg.

All commercials 30 secs.
Produced by The Partners' Film Company

1989
Client: Ontario Hydro
Titles: 'Timers', 'Hot Showers', 'Cleaners', 'Laundry'
Agency: Burghardt Wolowich Crunkhorn

1990
Client: William Neilson Ltd, Cadbury
Titles: 'Bistro', 'Surveillance'
Agency: Scali McCabe Sloves

Client: Nike International
Title: 'Transformation'
Agency: Wieden and Kennedy

Selected Sequels and Remakes
Scanners
When the original *Scanners* proved a success, producer Pierre David turned the property into a franchise. The new films shared little with the first one apart from their titles and the concept of the scanner. *Scanners II: The New Order* (1991) involves the offspring of characters from the original, but this is incidental in a film which mixes detective tropes, horror and politics, as a police commissioner tries to use scanners to pacify a city.

A third film, *Scanners III: Takeover* (also known as *Scanner Force*, 1992) involves a scanner turned into a maniac by a medical trial gone wrong. She tries to take over the world using a *Videodrome*-like TV signal, and, with shades of Vale and Revok, her brother must stop her. These were the first films directed by Christian Duguay, who would next make *Screamers*, an adaptation of Philip K. Dick's *Second Variety*. The *Scanners* sequels fail to live up to the potential of the idea and the franchise spun off into *Scanner Cop* (1994), directed by Pierre David himself. This was set in Los Angeles, where a scanner cop (or as one critic nicely put it, a police scanner) tries to stop a madman using mind control to set the local population against the police. A *Scanners* reboot movie and TV series, to be developed by Dimension Films, failed to materialise. The rights were then bought by new producers, who announced a series in 2017.

The Fly II

Mel Brooks and David Cronenberg had different ideas about a sequel to *The Fly*. When the director moved on, Brooksfilms hired the original film's make-up effects designer Chris Walas. In *The Fly II*, Ronnie gives birth to her son with Brundle, Martin. At first, the boy's insect nature manifests only as super abilities and an accelerated growth rate, which tops out conveniently when the actor mutates into Eric Stoltz. Martin matures in the tender care of Bartok industries, the shady corporation that funded his father's work. On behalf of the company, the boy revives his father's teleportation studies while he tries to find a cure for his appalling inheritance. But time is not on his side, for when the insect genes gain dominance, he will mutate into another Brundlefly. Daphne Zuniga plays his colleague Beth who becomes his girlfriend, setting the stage to revisit the emotional dynamics of the first film, with a traditional story of girl-meets-monster. John Getz makes an enjoyable cameo as Stathis Borans. With *The Fly II*, Brooks got his 'more of the same', and so did the audience, as the film regurgitates the nourishment it took from the original and sucks it up again for our entertainment. This is a fun, well-made horror if you can get over the looming superiority of the picture that gave birth to it. *The Fly II*, with its tagline 'Like father, like son,' succeeds as a B-movie. The story continues in a comic book, *The Fly: Outbreak*.

The Dead Zone – TV series

Not exactly a remake of Cronenberg's film, this was a relative of sorts, based on characters from the King novel. *The Dead Zone* (2002–2008) was developed by TV veterans Michael and Shawn Piller for the USA Network. The show starred Anthony Michael Hall as Johnny with Nicole de Boer as Sarah, and was a solidly entertaining mainstream drama with some of the original's sense of sadness. Due to falling ratings, the network cancelled *The Dead Zone* after season six and the show ended without a resolution.

The Fly – Opera

The Fly is an opera by Howard Shore, who composed new music for a libretto by David Henry Hwang. Directed by David Cronenberg and conducted by Plácido Domingo, it was commissioned jointly by the Théâtre du Châtelet, Paris, and the Los Angeles Opera. *The Fly* premiered in Paris on 3 July 2008 (as *La Mouche*) and opened in L.A. on 7 September. The opera takes the structure of the film and fuses it with elements of the short story, setting the action in the 1950s. It opens with Brundlefly dead, as Veronica talks to the police about the strange events that led to this moment. Critics were unimpressed. The French reviewers started joking about a 'bad buzz', and when *The Fly* reached Los Angeles, its Atlantic crossing had failed to improve its chances. The *New York Times* called Shore's music 'curiously tame'. The *L.A. Times* critic was 'at a loss to understand why *The Fly* has turned out so dreary, despite the inclusion of sex, nudity, puppetry and athleticism,' and given that Shore had scored the film itself 'effectively, even operatically'. The lead singers, Daniel Okulitch and Ruxandra Donose as Seth and Veronica respectively, came in for praise: Okulitch, for his delicacy and poignancy; Donose for her 'vulnerability, quiet intensity and lush colorings'. Dante Ferretti's 'strikingly intricate' set design was lauded, but the lighting was criticised as too dark to show off Stephan Dupuis's Brundlefly makeup design. The opera ends on a hopeful note with Veronica accepting her role as the mother of Brundlefly's larva, ushering in 'the new flesh'.

Eastern Promises II

In 2012, a sequel to *Eastern Promises* was proposed, with Viggo Mortensen, writer Steven Knight, and David Cronenberg all returning. The new story would follow Nikolai to Russia. When he and Focus Features couldn't agree on a budget, Cronenberg left the project. The script was repurposed as a standalone story, *Body Cross*, with William Oldroyd (Lady Macbeth) set to direct.

Rabid

Jen and Sylvia Soska, Canadian filmmakers known for *Dead Hooker in a Trunk* and *American Mary*, brought out a version of *Rabid* in 2019. They took it on because the film would be made with or without them and, as admirers of David Cronenberg, they didn't want to pass up the opportunity. The filmmakers placed quite a few easter eggs in their movie, some of which are distractingly self-conscious. For example, the surgeons treating Rose wear Mantle-red gowns; the institute is named after Burroughs, with Dr Keloid given a mention. A satire on gender roles and consumerism, the new film has important things to say about the fashion industry. *Rabid* takes the 1977 original as a starting point for a fun, drive-in gore-fest that was received with mixed reviews. Cronenberg approved of the new *Rabid*, telling the Soskas when they met him, 'The film ended up where it should have'.

The Fly – proposed

For many years, Fox had been mulling a remake of Cronenberg's *The Fly*. In 2009 *The Guardian* reported that the studio was in talks with the director himself. Not wanting simply to recreate his first version, he intended to develop a parallel story that examined 'the nature of flyness'. Disagreement on the budget caused the director to demur, and he worked on Howard Shore's opera instead. In 2017, a new film was in the works, to be directed and co-written by J. D. Dillard (*Sleight*). By 2019, although a script was written, production had yet to start. Dillard remains hopeful of making *The Fly* 'in a way that excites' him.

Shivers – proposed

A new version of *Shivers* was announced to be directed in 2014 by Danish filmmaker Rie Rasmussen. The press release quoted Quentin Tarantino as saying that 'Rie is a perfect choice to helm the remake of *Shivers*'. The film has yet to appear.

Dead Ringers

In August 2020, it was revealed that Annapurna would make *Dead Ringers* as a series for Amazon. Starring and produced by Rachel Weisz, the show will be written by Alice Birch, whose scripts for TV series *Normal People* (2020) earned her an Emmy. Weisz will play the Mantle twins as a pair of OB-gyns who are 'on a mission to change the way women give birth, starting with Manhattan'. It looks set to have a different tone and focus from Cronenberg's film, although the twins still share everything: 'drugs, lovers, and an unapologetic desire to do whatever it takes, including pushing the boundaries on medical ethics in an effort to challenge antiquated practices and bring women's healthcare to the forefront'. It will likely be marvellous but different. Our one hope is that the twins will still be called Bev and Ellie.

Unmade Projects

In a parallel universe, we'd be watching David Cronenberg's take on *We Can Remember It For You Wholesale* a.k.a. *Total Recall*. Many of his unmade movies were simply offers he turned down. Others, he spent considerable time on. Let's start with a dancing welder.

Yes, Dawn Steel at Paramount asked David Cronenberg to direct *Flashdance*. In an interview with *birth.movies.death* he revealed that she thought him 'the perfect guy for that picture'. The director, with commendable self-awareness, declined. 'I had to tell her that I would *destroy* that movie and not deliberately. Just by being me, I would destroy it.' *Top Gun* (1986) was also offered, but this subversive classic is all the better for having been made by the late, great Tony Scott.

Early in the 1980s, Lucasfilm offered *Revenge of the Jedi* (as was) to Cronenberg. Imagine the scene at Jabba's palace, or the Sarlacc pit. Those cannibals, the Ewoks, might have been slightly less cuddly. We can only speculate on what Lucasfilm expected of him, but bearing in mind that they had earlier asked David Lynch to do *Jedi*, was it possible that George Lucas really did want such a director for his film?

After *Videodrome*, Universal asked David Cronenberg if he had any ideas he would like to pursue for a mainstream movie. Cronenberg went away and wrote a comedy called *Six Legs*, about entomologists discovering an addictive insect on a Caribbean island, in a scenario that resembled *Ghostbusters* as three friends went around having creature-hunting adventures in a van with a bug logo on its side. Universal turned it down, and the director was in any case dissatisfied with the ending, thinking that he had rushed it.

Total Recall is perhaps Cronenberg's most well-known near miss. He spent a year writing drafts, only to be told that he'd done the Dick version, not the 'Raiders of the Lost Ark on Mars' movie that was required. It could have been the weirdest film ever made from a PKD story. Instead, it became a satirical Paul Verhoeven action vehicle for Arnold Schwarzenegger. A little of Cronenberg's input survives in the final film: the Martian mutants. He told Chris Rodley in *Cronenberg on Cronenberg* that the difference between what he wanted *Total Recall* to be and how it turned out gave him a migraine just thinking about it, like a needle piercing his eye. Cronenberg was also up for another film that Verhoeven went on to make: *Robocop* (1987).

He was attached for a time to *American Psycho*, which even its author Bret Easton Ellis thought impossible to film. Nonetheless, Ellis wrote a script in the early 1990s for Cronenberg, 'with a young actor attached named Brad Pitt', the writer told *Rolling Stone*. 'David was lovely – is lovely. I still like David – but he had strange demands. He hated shooting restaurant scenes, and he hated shooting nightclub scenes. And he didn't want to shoot the violence. I ignored everything he said. So, of course, he was disappointed with it and he hired his own writer; that script was worse for him and he dropped out.' *American Psycho* came to the screen in 2000 with Mary Harron directing a witty adaptation that she wrote with Genevieve Turner. Christian Bale is spot on as Ellis's antihero, Patrick Bateman. Brad Pitt would have been good, all the same.

Having signed on to *Basic Instinct 2*, David Cronenberg left the project in 2001 because of 'furious rows' with Sharon Stone. When the film was released, directed by Michael Caton-Jones and co-starring David Morrissey, it was panned.

In 2002, *Painkillers* was announced. This was the story of Saul Tenser, an artist with a high pain threshold, sent to infiltrate a subversive group. Inspired by *L'Art charnal*, a treatise by body modification artist Orlan, the film would have featured Orlan as herself, and Nicolas Cage as Tenser. Robert Lantos was set to produce. By the time the production was announced, Orlan had already had nine plastic surgery operations in a career of using 'her own body for artistic purposes'. But after years of living with his unmade, self-written screenplay, Cronenberg began to feel that he would be repeating himself, so he shelved the project. A pity: *Painkillers* had the potential to be disturbing and unique.

After completing *Crash*, Cronenberg tried to make *Red Cars*, a film about the Formula One championship at the 1961 Italian Grand Prix, and the rivalry between teammates Phil Hill and Wolfgang von Trips. When his car collided with another, von Trips was killed, as were fifteen spectators as the car crashed into them. The film was scuppered because of disagreements with the owner of Formula One, Bernie Ecclestone. In 2005, Cronenberg realised *Red Cars* as an art-book published by Volumina in an edition of 1,000 copies. The book contains the script of the unmade film, rare photographs from the Ferrari archives, unique artwork, and a model of a Ferrari 156. The cover was made of aluminium.

David Cronenberg considered Robert Ludlum's 1979 novel, *The Matarese Circle*, in 2008. MGM hoped to turn the book and its sequel into an espionage franchise starring Denzel Washington and Tom Cruise. When MGM went under, *The Matarese Circle* went with it. Meanwhile, Ludlum's Jason Bourne had started his run at Universal.

A move back into television could have been on the cards if the director had said yes to *True Detective*. He had been asked to helm the opener for the second season. Although he believed that these days TV is where 'the heat' is, he turned the show down. 'I considered it', he told an audience in 2015, 'but I thought that the script was bad, so I didn't do it. In TV, the director is just a traffic cop'. It seems fitting that the director of *Crash* should avoid becoming one of those.

Exhibitions and Retrospectives

There have been many retrospectives of David Cronenberg's work over the years. Here are some of them.

1983

Festival of Festivals, Toronto

This was the eighth outing for what would become known as the Toronto International Film Festival. As part of the festival, Piers Handling's retrospective of Cronenberg's cinema was the first to seriously consider the director as an artist, and produced the groundbreaking critical text, *The Shape of Rage*. Films screened: *Stereo*, *Crimes of the Future*, *Shivers*, *Rabid*, *Fast Company*, *The Brood*, *Scanners*, and *Videodrome*.

1993

The Strange Objects of David Cronenberg's Desire

Curated by Fern Bayer. An exhibition of 'drawings, objects and creatures', this opened first in Tokyo and was attended by huge crowds. A smaller version opened at the Royal Ontario Museum's Institute of Contemporary Culture in September the same year. In many ways, this is a precursor to TIFF's *Cronenberg Project*.

2008
Chromosomes: Cronenberg beyond cinema
Curated by Domenico De Gaetano and Luca Massimo Barbero
From 22 October to 16 November 2008, the Palazzo delle esposizioni hosted
Chromosomes, an exhibition of fifty images selected by Cronenberg from his
films, including *Scanners*, *Videodrome*, *The Fly*, *Dead Ringers*, *Naked Lunch*,
and others. Printed as fine-art works on canvas, these images were meant to
exist as autonomous objects outside their medium of origin. 2005's *Red Cars*
installation was included in the show, and the director discussed his work at a
Q&A session. The *Chromosomes* catalogue featured commentary from Viggo
Mortensen, William Gibson, Piers Handling and others. A short season of his
films accompanied the exhibition.

2013
The Cronenberg Project
Years in preparation, *The Cronenberg Project* is TIFF's multi-platform
celebration of the auteur's work. It launched in 2013 and continues today
online. Elements included the *Evolution* exhibition, a virtual museum, a
season of Cronenberg films projected from restored prints; gallery projects,
and a 'body mind change' web experience.

Evolution
2013–2017
Curated by Piers Handling and Noah Cowan, *Evolution* opened at the Bell
Light Box in Toronto, 1 November 2013 and ran until 19 January 2014. It then
toured Europe until 26 March 2017, stopping in the Netherlands, Italy, the
Czech Republic, and Poland. This featured photographs, drawings, text and
video, from *Stereo* to *Cosmopolis*. Many props were displayed, including the
telepod from *The Fly*, a Mugwump from *Naked Lunch*, and the gynaecological
instruments from *Dead Ringers*. The exhibition was divided into sections
covering Cronenberg's entire career in chronological order. Handling and
Cowan edited the excellent catalogue.

Transformations
5 September to 29 December 2013. An exhibition at the Museum of
Contemporary Art, Toronto, in which six artists were invited to respond to
a specific theme in Cronenberg's work: the desire humans have to evolve.
Organised by TIFF. The artists were: Candice Breitz, James Coupe, Marcel
Dzama, Jeremy Shaw, Jamie Shovlin, and Laurel Woodcock.

The Cronenberg Museum
An indispensable resource, recommended for essays, timeline, rare footage,
interviews and images: http://cronenbergmuseum.tiff.net

Body Mind Change
This immersive game experience is an online extension of the exhibition. It purports to come from a biotech company licensing the technology in Cronenberg's films, developing them for real. http://www.bodymindchange.ca/

2014
David Cronenberg THE EXHIBITION
At the EYE Film Institute, Amsterdam, 22 June to 14 September. An incarnation of the travelling *Evolution*. Cronenberg's short film *The Nest* was commissioned for this show. The Czech website for *Evolution* is here: http://www.cronenberg.cz/en/

Warhol
In 2006, at the Art Gallery of Ontario, David Cronenberg curated *Supernova: Stars, Death and Disasters, 1962–1964*, an exhibition about Andy Warhol.

Regular Collaborators
As well as using certain actors more than once, David Cronenberg has built solid relationships with key creatives behind the camera. Some of them were relatively inexperienced when they first worked with him, and others were already respected in their field. Each has contributed to the idea of what makes a Cronenberg film.

Costume Designer: Denise Cronenberg
Having been a ballet dancer and a fashion designer, Denise Cronenberg started in film as a wardrobe trainee on *Videodrome*. She worked on all her brother's feature films after that, as well as on his short, *Camera*. Initially credited as Denise Woodley, she graduated to wardrobe mistress on *The Dead Zone*. Her career as a professional costume designer began on *The Fly*. She gave the characters distinctive looks, from Brundle's tweed to Bill Lee's trenchcoat, to Vaughan's leather jacket, to Spider's drab old clothes. Of particular note are the blood-red surgical gowns she designed for the Mantles in *Dead Ringers*, expressing the ecclesiastical aspect of the operating theatre. David told the *Globe and Mail*, 'The twins viewed their roles as doctors as almost a religious thing, with an element of spirituality and philosophy. As soon as I said that to Denise, she immediately understood what I was talking about and what we needed'. She had a varied career in film and television, often in the genre of horror, including *Resident Evil: Afterlife*, Zack Snyder's *Dawn of the Dead* remake, and William Friedkin's *The Guardian*. Her other films included Agnieszka Holland's *The Third Miracle*, and her son Aaron Woodley's *Rhinoceros Eyes*. Denise Cronenberg passed away on 22 May 2020, at the age of 81.

Production Designer and Art Director: Carol Spier
Since *Fast Company*, on which she was as an art director, Carol Spier has

worked on every Cronenberg feature except *Spider* and *Cosmopolis*. In a distinguished career, she has won or been nominated for several Genie Awards, all but one of them for Cronenberg pictures. Her work is functional as well as ingenious. An example is the revolving set for *The Fly*, which allowed Brundle to walk on the ceiling. The set for the apartment-clinic in *Dead Ringers* coolly contained the Mantle twins' inner turmoil. Spier's design on *Naked Lunch* is particularly impressive, recreating Tangier on a soundstage in Toronto. The film won her a Genie for Best Art Direction, her second such win on a Cronenberg film, and not her last: she would also win for *eXistenZ*. Carol Spier has also designed for other films, including Guillermo del Toro's *Pacific Rim* and Lone Scherfig's *The Kindness of Strangers*.

Cinematographer: Mark Irwin

A fellow Canadian, Irwin had shot only three films when he started work with David Cronenberg. His first two movies with the auteur were *Fast Company* and *The Brood*. Irwin went on to shoot *Scanners*, *Videodrome*, *The Dead Zone* and *The Fly*. For the last three, he won the Canadian Society of Cinematographers award for Best Cinematography in a Theatrical Feature. Committed to filming *The Blob* for Chuck Russell, Irwin was unable to do *Dead Ringers*. He has since pursued a prolific and successful career on projects as diverse as comedies for the Farrelly brothers and *Wes Craven's New Nightmare* (1994).

Cinematographer: Peter Suschitzky

A British Director of Photography with a considerable career already behind him, Suschitzky became Cronenberg's new cinematographer on *Dead Ringers*. Himself the son of a cinematographer, Suschitzky started young. At 19 he began as a clapper boy and became a camera operator at 22. His first film as DP was *It Happened Here* (1964), the on-off nature of its production meaning that it took eight years to complete. Tending to choose projects that spoke to him artistically, he shot some notable films in the next two decades, including *The Rocky Horror Picture Show* (Jim Sharman, 1975), *Valentino* (Ken Russell, 1977) and *The Empire Strikes Back* (Irvin Kershner, 1980). Cronenberg, with characteristic bluntness, has said that the latter is the only one of the *Star Wars* movies that looks good. Suschitzky has also shot notable films for others, including Bernard Rose, Tim Burton and M. Night Shyamalan. Among his awards are four Genies, for *Dead Ringers*, *Naked Lunch*, *Crash* and *Eastern Promises*.

Editor: Ronald Sanders

There have been many famous editor-director duos in film. One of the most enduring is the partnership between David Cronenberg and Ronald Sanders, who has edited all of the director's features from *Fast Company* onwards. Sanders has won Genies for four of these: *Dead Ringers*, *Crash*, *eXistenZ* and

Eastern Promises. A graduate of the University of Manitoba, Sanders began with an amateur film produced in college. *Fast Company* was his second film as an editor. Other work includes *Coraline*, Henry Selick's 2009 stop-motion animation from Neil Gaiman's book. Sanders edited Viggo Mortensen's *Falling* (2020), in which his sometime director takes an acting role.

Composer: Howard Shore

Howard Shore's music has been an essential part of Cronenberg's filmic identity for decades. His music for *The Brood*, only the second film of his career, is full of Hitchcockian menace. Because of him, *The Fly* sounds like the great science fiction films of the 1950s. The music for *Dead Ringers* is appropriately elegiac, its main title being one of Shore's best. *Naked Lunch* goes all Bebop-on-acid, with help from Ornette Coleman. *Crash* is twisted metal guitar and sharp angles. *Spider*'s music, performed by the Kronos Quartet along with soloists, feels fragile and sacred, church music for a deconsecrated mind. Aside from his Cronenberg collaborations, Shore created epic, Oscar-winning music for Peter Jackson's Middle Earth epics, scores for several David Fincher films; and many others in a remarkable career. He has written a concerto for Lang Lang, his collaborator on *A Dangerous Method*; a symphony based on his *Lord of the Rings* music; as well as other orchestral pieces, and works for guitar. In 2008, his opera based on *The Fly*, premiered in Paris, with libretto by David Henry Hwang and directed by Cronenberg. Shore's music for Cronenberg is worth seeking out on disc. Starting in 2016, Mondo released vinyl LPs of the scores to *Dead Ringers, Crash, The Brood/Scanners* and *Naked Lunch,* all with superb cover artwork. Shore also released *Dead Ringers, Naked Lunch* and *Crash* on CD, through his own label, Howe Records.

The Brood: The Next Generation

David Cronenberg's children have pursued careers in the creative arts, working variously in film, photography, fiction and other disciplines.

Cassandra Cronenberg (born 1972) is the child of David's first marriage, to Margaret Hindson. Cassandra is a director, producer, actor and screenwriter. Outside film, she is a painter, a novelist and a yogi. She gained her Honours BA in East Asian Studies from McGill University and her BA in Psychology from York University. She trained as an assistant director on her father's films *Naked Lunch*, *M. Butterfly* and *Crash*, as well as on Michael Apted's *Extreme Measures* (1996), in which her father played a lawyer. Now a fully trained assistant director, she worked on *eXistenZ*, and on films by Canadian directors Mary Harron (*American Psycho*) and Atom Egoyan (*The Sweet Hereafter*). In 2013, she wrote, produced, directed and acted in a short film, *Candy*, which premiered at the Toronto International Film Festival. Cassandra's novella *Down the Street* came out in 2014 from Quattro Books.

Brandon Cronenberg (born 1980) is David's son with Carolyn Zeifman. Until his early twenties, he considered himself 'a book nerd not a cinephile'. On realising that he wanted to make cinema, he enrolled in Ryerson University, Toronto, to study film. His first feature, *Antiviral*, is a satire on the cult of celebrity. It debuted at Cannes in *Un Certain Regard* in 2012, alongside his father's film, *Cosmopolis*. Brandon re-edited *Antiviral* to tighten it before its wider release. A nine-minute short followed in 2019, *Please Speak Continuously and Describe Your Experiences as They Come to You*. This also opened at Cannes, and was included in TIFF's annual list of Canada's Top Ten short films. His second feature, *Possessor*, opened in 2020 to positive reviews.

Caitlin Cronenberg (born 1984) is David's daughter with Carolyn Zeifman. She worked as a stills photographer on *Cosmopolis*, as well as on Denis Villeneuve's *Enemy* (2013) and Paul W. S. Anderson's *Pompeii* (2014). She is a fine-art photographer, and shoots commercially for fashion brands and magazines. Her photography has been shown in gallery exhibitions, and bought for private collections. Caitlin has published two books. *Poser* (2010) is a collection of intimate monochrome photographs of men and women. She writes that their appearance in the book forms a bond between them, as they all posed nude for the same woman. Her second book is *The Endings* (2014), featuring stories of breakups, as interpreted in compositions featuring well-known actresses. The book was art-directed by Jessica Ennis, with whom Caitlin co-directed a short film to accompany it. The cover she shot for Drake's album *Views* (2016) went viral. It portrays the artist enlarged and sitting on top of the CN Tower in Toronto, his legs dangling. Also a director of music videos, Caitlin made an animated photo-based promo for Canadian artist Hill/Brenna MacQuarrie.

Selected Awards And Honours

David Cronenberg and his films have received around 150 nominations, awards and honours. The following is a selective list of his wins.

1983
Fantasporto International Fantasy Film Award. *Scanners*: Best Film.
Cannes Film Festival. *Videodrome*: Best Director.

1984
Avoriaz Fantastic Film Festival. *The Dead Zone*: Suspense Award, Critics Award, Antennae II Award.

Brussels International Festival of Fantasy Film. *Videodrome*. Best Science Fiction film (tied).

Fantafestival. *The Dead Zone*: Audience Award, Best Film.

1987
Avoriaz. *The Fly*: Special Jury Award.

1988
Cannes. *Dead Ringers*: Best Picture, Best Director, Best Screenplay.

1989
Avoriaz. *Dead Ringers*: Grand Prize; C.S.T. Award.

1991
Cannes. *Naked Lunch*: Best Director, Best Screenplay.

New York Film Critics Circle Awards. *Naked Lunch*: Best Screenplay.

1992
National Society of Film Critics Awards, US *Naked Lunch*: Best Director, Best Screenplay.

1996
Cannes. *Crash*: Special Jury Prize. Winner, Best Screenplay.

Cahiers du Cinéma. *Crash*: Top 10 Film Award.

1999
Berlin International Film Festival. *eXistenZ*: Silver Bear.

Amsterdam Fantastic Film Festival. *eXistenZ*: Silver Scream Award.

2002
Directors Guild of Canada. *Spider*: Craft Award, Direction – Feature Film.

Ghent International Film Festival: Special Jury Prize for his body of work.

2003
Cannes. *Spider*: Best Director.

2006
International Cinephile Society Awards. *A History of Violence*: Best Director.

2008
Fotogramas de Plata. *Eastern Promises*: Best Foreign Film.

Directors Guild of Canada. *Eastern Promises*: Craft Award, Direction – Feature Film.

2012
Directors Guild of Canada. *A Dangerous Method*: Craft Award, Direction – Feature Film.

Vancouver Film Critics Circle. *A Dangerous Method*: Best Director – Canadian Film.

2014
Provincetown International Film Festival. 'Filmmaker on the Edge' Award.

Personal awards
1999
Inducted into Canada's Walk of Fame.

Governor General's Performing Arts Award.

2002
Officer of the Order of Canada.

2005
Stockholm Film Festival. Lifetime Achievement Award.

2006
Cannes. *Carrosse d'Or* (Lifetime Achievement Award).

2007
Hamburg Film Festival. Douglas Sirk Award.

2009
Légion d'honneur, France.

2010
Honorary patron of the Philosophical Society, Trinity College, Dublin.

2011
Gotham Awards. Tribute Awards.

2012
Queen Elizabeth II Diamond Jubilee medal.

2014
Member of the Order of Ontario.
Companion of the Order of Canada.

2015
Directors Guild of Canada. Lifetime Achievement Award.

2018
Venice International Film Festival. Honorary Golden Lion.

Further Exploration and Bibliography

From academic studies to biographies and collections of interviews, the books listed here are recommended. Some may be out of print but available secondhand. David Cronenberg's own writings are of primary interest; the Rodley and Grünberg books are a fine place to start. To reiterate the spoiler warning given at the beginning, you may prefer to watch first, read later.

Interviews

Rodley, C., (ed.) *Cronenberg on Cronenberg* (Faber & Faber, 1992)
Grünberg, S., *David Cronenberg: Interviews with Serge Grünberg* (Plexus Publishing, 2005)

Studies

Handling, P., (ed.) *The Shape of Rage: The Cinema of David Cronenberg* (New York Zoetrope, 1983)
Silverberg, I., (ed.) *Everything is Permitted: The Making of Naked Lunch* (HarperCollins, 1992)
Morris, P., *David Cronenberg – A Delicate Balance* (ECW, 1993)
Costello, J., *David Cronenberg* (Pocket Essentials, 2000)
Arthur, J.; Barker, M.; Harindranath, R., *The Crash Controversy* (Wallflower Press, 2001)
Beard, W., *The Artist as Monster: The Cinema of David Cronenberg* (University of Toronto Press, 2006)
Mathijs, E., *The Cinema of David Cronenberg* (Wallflower Press, 2008)
Handling, P.; Cowan, N., *David Cronenberg Evolution* (TIFF exhibition catalogue, 2013)
Bissette, S., *The Brood*, (Electric Dreamhouse, an imprint of P.S. Publishing, 2020)

Books by David Cronenberg

Crash (Screenplay) (Faber and Faber, 1996)
eXistenZ: a Graphic Novel (with Scoffield S., illustrator) (Key Porter Books, 1999)
Collected Screenplays 1: Stereo, Crimes of the Future, Shivers, Rabid (Faber and Faber, 2002)
Red Cars (Volumina Artbooks, 2005)
Consumed (novel, Scribner, 2014)

Other Resources

David Cronenberg's entry at the Canadian Encyclopedia:
https://www.thecanadianencyclopedia.ca/en/article/david-cronenberg
The Senses of Cinema overview of Cronenberg's career up to *Spider:*
http://sensesofcinema.com/2002/great-directors/cronenberg/

Film Sources (by first publication)

King, S., *The Dead Zone* (Viking Press, 1979)

Langelaan, G., *The Fly* (*Playboy* magazine, June 1957)

Burroughs, W. S., *Naked Lunch* (Olympia Press, France, 1959; Grove Press, US, 1962)

Ballard, J. G., *Crash* (Cape, 1973)

Wood, B.; Geasland, J., *Twins* (Signet, 1978)

Hwang, D. H., *M. Butterfly* (play, National Theatre, Washington D.C., 1988; Plume, 1989)

McGrath, P., *Spider* (Penguin, 1990)

Wagner, J.; Locke, V., *A History of Violence* (Paradox Press, 1997)

DeLillo, D., *Cosmopolis*, (Scribner, 2003)

Hampton C., *The Talking Cure* (play, Cottesloe Theatre, London, 2003; Faber and Faber, 2003)

Kerr, J., *A Most Dangerous Method* (Knopf, 1993)

Wagner, B., *Dead Stars* (Penguin, 2012). Not strictly an adaptation; listed because of its relationship to *Maps to the Stars*.